SUTHERLAND BIRDS

Royalties from the sale of this work will be devoted to
wildlife research in Sutherland

FIRST PUBLISHED 1983

SUTHERLAND BIRDS

A Guide to the Status and Ecology of Birds
in Sutherland District

Edited by
STEWART ANGUS

ESTABLISHED
1899

THE NORTHERN TIMES LIMITED

Published and printed by
The Northern Times Limited,
Main Street, Golspie, Sutherland

ISBN 0 9501718 3 2

Acknowledgements

As Editor, I would like to convey my gratitude to Donnie Macdonald, Desmond Nethersole-Thompson, Ian Pennie and David Whitaker, the major contributors to the introductory sections, not only for their own chapters, but for their valued advice on the remainder of the text.

Such a guide cannot be produced without the help of a great number of people. Special thanks are due to John Barrett for wader figures, Donald Bremner for details of raptors, and to Roger Broad, Roy Dennis, Derek Langslow and Maimie Nethersole-Thompson for their helpful comments on the text.

Thanks are also due to Eric Hosking FRPS for his spectacular cover picture, to G G and I M Bates, Ray Collier, Ian Pennie, Sandy Sutherland, David Whitaker and the Nature Conservancy Council for photographs, to Sally Orr and David Whitaker for drawings, to Katalin Svehla for the map, and to Mrs Ellen Munro for typing.

All contributors and photographers have given their material gratis so that the royalties from sales may be used to sponsor further wildlife research in Sutherland.

Contents

Views expressed in this publication are not necessarily those of any organisations with which the contributors may be associated.

TABLE OF ILLUSTRATIONS

* These are the only photographs in this book which were not taken in Sutherland.

Introduction

Sutherland has much to offer the bird-watcher. Many of the more spectacular birds of the Highlands may be seen amid equally spectacular scenery.

This guide owes much to the pioneer workers of the nineteenth century who produced the first detailed accounts of Sutherland's birds. Selby was the first of these, touring the north and west in 1834 using 'a light boat suspended upon a four-wheeled carriage'. St. John followed in 1848, and is remembered today as one of those chiefly responsible for the extermination of the Osprey. Perhaps the greatest of them all were Harvie-Brown and Buckley, who between them produced remarkably detailed accounts of the birds, mammals, reptiles, amphibians and fish of much of the north of Scotland. Ian Pennie, one of the contributors to this guide, gives a more detailed account of the early workers in his section of *The Sutherland Book,* where he also gives the only recent list of Sutherland's birds.

This guide attempts to give a comprehensive account of the status of birds in Sutherland District up to 1982, listing all species for which there are accepted records from the 20th century, together with some of the more interesting historical records.

Owing to local government boundary revisions in 1975 and 1977, it is perhaps necessary to point out that Sutherland District includes the parishes of Tongue, Farr and Kincardine (though for the purposes of most biological recording Kincardine remains in Ross-shire!).

Sutherland is a very large area, covering 448,680 hectares (1,108,707 acres). The climatic influences of three coasts and the exceptionally varied geology combine to produce a wide range of habitats.

Birds should not be looked at in isolation, and the importance of these habitats to our avifauna is outlined in four chapters, all written by experienced local ornithologists who know their fields intimately. A fifth chapter is devoted to ornithological conservation in the District.

A gazetteer of the less well-known place names used in the guide is provided for those less familiar with the District together with a map.

The bibliography is highly selective, being restricted to the most relevant publications and those quoted in the guide. In general works dealing with single species have been omitted from this list.

The species list follows the order and nomenclature of Voous (1977). The terms used to describe status are those thought to describe the situation most accurately, and should not be interpreted too literally. The movements of some birds are very complex and cannot be described with absolute accuracy within a few lines. Likewise the limits (apart from actual dates) of stay for visiting species are intended only as a guide, and records may occasionally occur outside these limits.

The systematic list was compiled from Baxter and Rintoul (1953), Scottish Bird Reports, and all available papers, reports and notes, including the personal records of all the contributors. Many records, particularly of numbers, are published for the first time. Unfortunately, some of the figures given are now rather out of date, notably those of Rook/Jackdaw winter roosts and those of Operation Seafarer.

No reference is made to rejected records, even where these have been published, except in the case of the Willow Tit. Almost all the records given here have been passed through the 'official system' based on county recorders. One very experienced ornithologist who does not use this system has contributed records to the guide. Where these records are in any way unusual, their 'unofficial' status is specified.

Where there are several recent records of scarcer species, older records (before 1950 or even 1960) are often omitted.

The list contains details of 262 species, four of which have not been recorded in the 20th century. Of the 258 which make up the 'recent' list, one (Red-legged Partridge) is a recent introduction, and at least three are probable 'escapes'.

121 species breed regularly, and a further 22 have bred occasionally (some only once) or no longer breed regularly. The latter figure includes the White-tailed Eagle, which last bred in 1901; the Magpie which last bred in 1920, and the Corn Bunting, which last bred around 1970.

It will be seen from the list that a number of species are known to be vulnerable to severe winters. In the winter of 1981-82 there were about six weeks of unabated very low temperatures, so that many birds either moved out or succumbed, probably due more to a lack of food than the actual cold. Some sources of food, such as the marine invertebrates which are so important to wintering waders and wildfowl, may take years to build up to their former level of availability, so that it could be a long time before the birds which rely on them for food recover.

Tourism is important to the economy of Sutherland, and birds contribute a great deal to the attraction the District holds for visitors. Please remember that some birds are vulnerable to disturbance, and help to ensure that the birds you see will be there for others to see the following year.

All possible steps have been taken to ensure that the text is accurate, but bird populations do not remain static. The Editor would appreciate any additions or corrections. It is hoped that this volume will act as a stimulus to recording, so that we may obtain a more detailed and accurate picture of our bird fauna.

Eider: duck (left) and two drakes

10

The East Coast and Eastern Lowlands

by D. Macdonald

In its diversity of habitats the south-east of Sutherland far outstrips other areas of the District. Even the coastline presents a variety of outstanding features ranging through the mudflats of the Dornoch Firth with their adjoining patches of salt marsh; extensive stretches of sandy beaches interspersed here and there with rocks, and backed by marram dunes and links; the superb salt water basin of Loch Fleet; and at the extreme north end a small portion of coastal cliffs at the Ord of Caithness.

Autumn and winter are, perhaps, the best seasons for bird-watching on the coast when the sea duck and wader populations reach peak numbers. An Eider raft, sometimes numbering up to 3000 birds, can usually be seen off the bar at the entrance to Loch Fleet and, if one is lucky, the sighting of a King Eider may be obtained, as since 1973 at least two have accompanied common Eider flocks feeding in the Loch Fleet or Embo Pier areas. Recently, a winter roost of up to 4000 Long-tailed Ducks has been discovered off the coast at Brora.

This coastline attracts large numbers of common waders and, particularly during August and September, some less common species such as Little Stint, Curlew Sandpiper, Ruff, Black-tailed Godwit, Spotted Redshank, Green and Wood Sandpipers. Here, too, have been sighted four Nearctic waders — White-rumped Sandpiper, Stilt Sandpiper, Buff-breasted Sandpiper and Lesser Yellowlegs. The Stilt Sandpiper was the first Scottish record and first British spring record. The last point is of particular interest as the species migrates chiefly west of the Mississippi and is less common on the Atlantic coast where it appears chiefly in autumn. A wader whose over-wintering numbers have considerably increased in recent years is the Grey Plover. Annually, since 1946, when it was first discovered, is a Sandwich Tern roost about 1 mile west of Dornoch Point. The birds arrive in early April, build up to about 500 in number, and disperse in mid May, presumably to some breeding site.

Apart from isolated areas of agricultural land scattered, here and there, in the interior and on the coast of the north and west, the main concentration of the District's arable land is confined to a narrow strip extending along the east coast. In general the farms are situated on the lower ground adjoining the shoreline while crofts of varying size merge into the uplands. Barley and oats are the chief cereal crops but wheat is also grown occasionally; root crops include potatoes, swedes and turnips. Hay has always been the staple grass crop, but in recent years there has been a tendency to cut grass for silage, the earlier cutting of which may have a harmful effect on ground-nesting birds.

Unlike many extensive arable areas, which tend to look rather featureless, the agricultural strip of south-east Sutherland, owing to its diversity of landscape, is of particular attraction to the ornithologist. Breaking the continuity of arable farmland are several villages with their colourful cottage gardens, a county burgh with distinctive architectural charm, deciduous and coniferous woods and the stately, parkland policies of Skibo and Dunrobin Castles. Moreover, on one side, the moors and mountains of the vast hinterland are always visible while, on the other hand, stretches the sea.

Autumn through to early spring is, perhaps, the best time for observing birds on farmland. It is then that the stubbles and pastures attract numerous species including wildfowl, waders, pigeons, corvids and the winter thrushes, while a variety of seed bearing plants, growing by the unkempt field edges, entice finches and buntings. In early March the lapwings return to their breeding haunts in the marshy fields. Is there anything more evocative of springtime than the call and flight display of the Lapwing when heard at dusk on a March evening? The Redshank also breeds in the same habitat. Within the past few decades the Oystercatcher has taken to breeding on farm pastures, sometimes even nesting in young cereal crops and, more recently, the Curlew has become a convert to nesting in pasture fields. Two bird voices primarily associated with springtime on well cultivated land are the 'rusty-gate' call of the Grey Partridge at even-fall and the song of the Skylark, . . . *who sings for joy, seeing Spring over Winter's shoulder* (Sylvia Lynd).

In recent times two species have been lost to farmland. The

Corncrake, whose rasping note was once a familiar voice of summer nights, has gone from all its old haunts. Its departure has been one of a slow decline over a period of at least forty years and, although rarely heard now in South-east Sutherland, it still lingers on in ever-diminishing numbers on the west coast. The disappearance of the Corn Bunting has been much more eventful. In the area between the Meikle Ferry and Loch Fleet it was estimated that there were at least twenty breeding pairs during the early 1960s, but by 1970 a sudden and rapid decline had set in and only four sightings of single birds were obtained between 1972 and 1982, the last being in 1976. This decline has been widespread and has been recorded from Shetland southwards.

Partially to offset those losses there has appeared one new arrival — the Collared Dove which, since it was first recorded at Dornoch in April 1964, has become a familiar denizen of many gardens, farm steadings and agricultural lands. So rapid has been its increase that by the end of 1966 a flock of up to 60 birds could be observed feeding on the stubbles. Recently its numbers appear to have stabilized.

Frequently lying adjacent to farmland and gardens are areas of rough scrub. Generally, they consist of a few small trees, some whin or broom bushes, a varied assortment of wild roses, brambles and wild raspberries with a thick undergrowth of either bracken or tall weeds. Those miniature jungles are a favourite resort of our three commonest warblers — Sedge Warbler, Whitethroat and Willow Warbler — as well as of several resident species. In short those delectable spots are an ideal habitat for small passerines but, in recent years, many have been lost through development, so that they are decreasing at an alarming rate.

Of the 31 Sutherland rookeries which contained 2110 nests in the 1975 census only three are outwith the area. The two largest were the Earl's Cross Wood rookery at Dornoch and Invershin rookery which held 401 and 330 nests respectively. Until recently a colony of Tree Sparrows nested in the foundations of the Rooks' nests at Earl's Cross Wood. South-east Sutherland is a prime area to observe how the Carrion Crow advances while the Hoodie slowly retreats northwards. Around the extreme south-east corner of the area it is now rare to see a pure Hoodie, all birds being either Carrions or hybrids.

The interior of the area consists mainly of vast stretches of moorland and mountain interspersed with wide straths and narrow glens. Flowing through most of these are some renowned salmon rivers including the Helmsdale, Brora, Cassley, Oykel and Carron. Fulmars now nest several miles inland up some of those straths, sharing the cliffs with Buzzards, Kestrels, Peregrines and Ravens. Glen Loth and Dunrobin Glen give one the impression of being remote and isolated and more akin to the wilder parts of

Sutherland, yet both are within a stone's throw of the coast. Golden Eagle, Merlin and Peregrine haunt their cliffs and hillsides.

Standing on The Mound embankment one is surrounded by a wonderful panorama of wildlife and scenic grandeur. On the inland side are The Mound Alderwoods, a quite unique reserve of the Nature Conservancy Council and a paradise for wildfowl. In winter it is a favoured haunt of Whooper Swans. Complementing the N.C.C. Reserve is, on the coastal side, the Scottish Wildlife Trust Reserve, comprising the Loch Fleet basin, Balblair, Ferry and Ferry Links Woods. Until recently a colony of Herring Gulls nested in the middle of mature Scots pines in Ferry Links Wood.

Skibo Estuary, with Lochs Evelix and Ospisdale and the mixed surrounding woods, is yet another delectable spot. The estuary is noted for Teal which in late autumn can number up to 1200 birds. Tufted Ducks and Coots are two species which can be seen at most times on the lochs. Two interesting denizens of the woods are the Great Spotted Woodpecker, a colonizer from further south in the last half-century, and the Capercaillie, a re-introduced species which, unfortunately, has become scarce in recent years. Further up the Firth is the Spinningdale/Ledmore oak wood, probably the best wood in Sutherland for summer migrants. It is the main haunt of the Wood Warbler, that delightful leaf warbler with the tremulous, ecstatic trill, which W. H. Hudson described as " the woodland sound which is like no other." On more than one occasion a Blackcap has been heard singing in the grounds of Spinningdale House. Inland from the wood is Spinningdale Bog where adult Greenshanks sometimes bring their young after hatching. Still further inland is Loch Migdale and the imposing inland cliff of Migdale Rock.

The Kyle of Sutherland (Page 17) is another splendid wildfowl refuge. Some distance up Strath Carron between Amat and Glencalvie is a small remnant of the old Caledonian Forest (Page 21). Running parallel and to the north of Strath Carron is Strath Oykel where there are extensive marshes on the north bank of the river. This area might, at any time, produce something of unusual interest to the ornithologist. Entering the Oykel from a north-westerly direction is the River Cassley which flows through Glen Cassley, perhaps the most attractive glen in all Sutherland. A short distance up from the entrance to the glen is the Achness Falls, an enchanting place if ever there was one. Here the river sweeps through a wooded gorge, falling over a double cataract. In a grassy hollow below the falls is an ancient little graveyard sheltered by a plantation of mature beech trees. Lord Grey of Falloden, Foreign Secretary during the early years of World War I, who rented the salmon fishing on the lower Cassley in the early years of the century, refers to this delectable spot in his book *Fly Fishing* as a "fine, fascinating and beautiful place" and he also describes the unique Scots pine growing out of a bare rock which stands in midstream at the falls, the description being enhanced by Eric Daglish's charming woodcut of the tree in moonlight. To delight the bird-watcher Grey Wagtails and Dippers are usually flitting about the falls.

Further up the glen as the road emerges from the lower woods on to the moors one becomes instantly aware of the distant twin-peaked massif of Ben More Assynt. Whether rising majestically into a clear blue sky or partly obscured as coils of mist sweep over its corries, this superb mountain dominates the upper reaches of the Cassley and is, perhaps, the best place to say farewell to South-east Sutherland.

The North and West Coasts

by Ian D. Pennie

The march with Caithness is Drum Hollistan: from here west a coastal strip of the Old Red Sandstone of Caithness extends to Strathy: fine cliff scenery with a few scattered colonies of auks and cormorants, but nothing comparable with the magnificent Torridonian Sandstone bird-cliffs of the Clo Mor and Handa. For migration studies on the other hand this piece of coastline is of great importance: at Strathy Point in November 1931 occured the greatest immigration of Snow Buntings ever recorded, tens of thousands of birds arriving like a snowstorm and covering the moorland like snowdrifts. Recent trapping studies round Melvich have shown a regular passage of small passerines, especially warblers, and have added Yellow-browed and Icterine Warblers to the Sutherland list. Records from Strathy Point and Farr Point indicate that these are potentially good spots for sea-watching. West again, Torrisdale Bay receives the waters of the Naver and Borgie rivers: for the bird-watcher the west side of the Borgie mouth, below Torrisdale township is well worth a visit especially during the autumn wader migration although neither here nor on the clean sands of the Kyle of Tongue do we find numbers of birds to compare with the estuaries and inlets of the east coast.

Offshore from the Kyle of Tongue, alluring but hard of access lies Island Roan — in reality a group of three islands, Eilean nan Ron, Eilean Iosal and Meall Halm. These are outliers of Old Red conglomerate which does not form good bird ledges and whether

The Kyle of Sutherland, an area favoured by wildfowl at all times of year.
Stewart Angus/NCC

The seabird cliffs of Handa.   *Ian D Pennie*

for this reason or not the cliffs are disappointingly poor in birds. For the favoured few however this island group holds a large Storm Petrel colony, and Great Skuas have become established breeders in recent years. The main island has a deserted village, evacuated in the 1930s and has since become a wintering ground for Barnacle Geese. These, together with the Barnacles of Eilean Hoan, Handa and Badcall are Greenland breeders, the Spitsbergen Barnacles wintering separately on the Solway. It is not necessary however to make the crossing to see the geese as it is possible to identify and count them with a telescope from the adjacent mainland.

Although the Kyle of Tongue cannot compare with the east-coast firths for birds it is a place of spectacular beauty, greatly enhanced by the magnificently engineered new causeway which might almost have been designed for bird and seal watchers. The great Moine peninsula, whence was named the Moine Schist, vast and remote, will reward the energetic walker with spectacular cliff scenery but, Fulmars apart, he will have to work hard for his birds: a pair of Peregrines on the cliffs perhaps, Skuas possibly and many breeding Dunlin and Redthroats, but in this sort of terrain one must never overlook the possibility of summer records of Sanderling, Turnstone or Purple Sandpiper. Gannets are common offshore and from any high point on this part of the coast on a clear day the twin islands of Stack and Skerry may be seen on the northern horizon with gannetry and lighthouse respectively.

West again round relatively birdless Eriboll to the lime-rich grasslands of Durness and Balnakeil, and a different world! Leaving the coast for a short time the birdwatcher should have at least a brief look at the four limestone lochs for ducks, of species unusual and unexpected in these parts, before leaving his car at Balnakiel car park and walking along the Balnakiel sands to Faraid Head. On the grassy slopes of the east side of Faraid is the only Puffin colony on the coast where with reasonable care it is possible to get close to the birds.

Across the Kyle of Durness a Minibus runs from Keoldale Ferry to Cape Wrath lighthouse and the Clo Mor (Page 25) — the Great Web of Cloth — as it appeared from the sea to former mariners. Here are the famous Torridonian sandstone bird-cliffs, the highest cliffs on the Scottish mainland with their vast and uncountable colonies of Puffins, Razorbills, Guillomots, Fulmars and Kittiwakes. The serious and energetic bird-watcher should leave the minibus at the Kearvaig track, walk to Kearvaig and, approaching the Clo Mor from the west follow the cliff-top eastwards for about three miles, skirting the east side of Sgribhis-bheinn (pronounced "Skreesh-ven") to be picked up by the Minibus (prior arrangement!) at Inshore. This is a tough walk but a memorable one.

From Cape Wrath southwards the cliffs, though imposing, have no significant bird colonies — apart from inaccessible Bulgach Island — until Handa is reached. Handa Island (Page 17),

18

its human population evacuated in 1849, is a Torridonian outlier from a rugged coastline of Lewisian Gneiss: the Mecca for west-coast bird-watching visitors it is almost too well known to require description. The island is a R.S.P.B. reserve with a summer warden and is approached by boat from Tarbet. The cliffs and bird colonies are scarcely less impressive than those of the Clo Mor (though many fewer Puffins) but there is the added bonus of breeding Great and Arctic Skuas.

South-west of Handa lies Point of Stoer, a Torridonian Sandstone headland with its stack "The Old Man of Stoer" and a few small auk colonies. Between the two is Eddrachillis Bay, beset with islands but alas, like those of Loch Laxford they are of little ornithological significance. The Grey-lags which formerly bred have all gone, the presence of Storm-Petrels uncertain, but the most interesting feature of several of these islands and adjacent mainland cliffs is the number of cliff-nesting Herons — no large heronries but small groups scattered along the coast from Loch Inchard to the Assynt shore. A large stick nest on a cliff ledge in these parts is much more likely to be a Heron's than an Eagle's.

To do justice to our coastline in such a short space is impossible. The cliff scenery is magnificent, the really spectacular bird colonies few and far between, but parts of the coast are seldom visited and little recorded with many opportunities for original observation and new discoveries.

Eagle and Peregrine country in the north-west. *Ian D Pennie*

Pool systems at the centre of remoter bogs are the breeding grounds of some of our more interesting wildfowl and waders. *Ian D Pennie*

A large inland loch — ideal Black-throated Diver habitat.   *David S Whitaker*

Amat Wood, the last large block of native pinewood in Sutherland.
Stewart Angus/NCC

Peatlands, Open Waters and Uplands

by Desmond Nethersole-Thompson

From the early 1830s onwards the great bog of Sutherland, with its flows, lochs and peatlands, has challenged and attracted naturalists. I well remember how small I felt when I first went north in 1932 to hunt for the elusive Greenshank in Strath Helmsdale.

In the north-east there are huge expanses of blanket bog between the Rivers Dyke and Helmsdale, with several large lochs and innumerable deep pools and dubhlochans. On the south side of the road between Badanloch and Syre there are grand lochs and, on both sides, miles of wild bogs and flows stretching from horizon to horizon. Young man's country, almost frightening in its sterility and challenge! Between Dalchork and Tongue, to west and east of the road, deer-grass dominates the immense peatlands. In the last 20 years some bogs have been drained and many acres of conifers planted. These dense plantations often block out dramatic landscapes, but they have attracted Hen Harriers and Short-eared Owls which nest until the trees grow taller. Between Loch Naver, Ben Hope and Loch Loyal there is another vast undulating sweep of flowland containing many lochs and dubhlochans around which the Old Naturalists so often hunted for greenshanks and divers. On both sides of the formidable Foinaven there are almost endless boulder-shot bogs in the gneiss, often with erratics perched on blocks of rock, some as large as small houses. In the south-east the peatlands are more gentle and undulating but there are many rolling tracts of deer grass with lochs and small islands which always

22

have a fascination for ornithologists. In the western flows of the deer grass country there are still many discoveries to be made between Oykel and Suilven, that marvellous spire of Torridonian sandstone. These, and other parts of the great bog of Sutherland, are the headquarters of the Greenshank which egg collectors and biologists have studied with delight and hunted with zest throughout this century.

These peatlands are also famous for their divers. How wonderful to watch the thrilling nuptial chase of Black-throated Divers high in air before the pair has definitely settled on a nest-site. But no one in Scotland has yet made a full study of the courtship, displays, sex-life and breeding behaviour of these magnificent birds. The summer life of the smaller Red-throated Diver is much better known, but there is always something almost incredibly evocative in the eerie chorus of wails and roll-growls in the evening as you crouch beside a rock overlooking the flow while waiting for a pair of Greenshanks to change-over at the nest. Black-throats usually prefer to lay their eggs on islands and edges of larger lochs (Page 21) and red-throats on tarns and pools far out in the flow. In north Sutherland, however, this pattern is sometimes reversed, with the black-throats choosing tiny pools whereas a few red-throats nest on islands or on the edges of large lochs.

Sometimes there are rarities. A Pectoral Sandpiper, a North American wader, displayed over a flow on the marches of Sutherland and Caithness. While the display took place on Caithness side of the District boundary, it was visible from Sutherland. Temminck's Stints are always possible finds. In 1962 I met with an undoubted nesting bird on the edge of a huge flow. Friends have found isolated pairs of dainty Red-necked Phalaropes nesting in quite acidic tarns, but on the Scottish mainland these beauties are few. Whimbrels have occasionally bred on the flows and grass-heaths but they are not true birds of the squashy peat-bogs.

Between 1968-72 we studied Wood Sandpipers in grassy peatland close to a loch in north Sutherland. It was wonderful to listen to the yodelling songs of the the cock and in 1969 to find a nest by watching the pair change duties. This exciting loch was one of the few places in Sutherland where Greenshank and Redshank shared different parts of the same flow. Dunlin, Curlew and Golden Plover all nested on the adjacent peatlands, and in 1968 a pair of Green Sandpipers fed by the lochside. A pair of Black-throated Divers had eggs beside the loch and red-throats laid close to tiny pools in a wet flow.

Dunlins usually nest in small groups or clusters among complexes of dubhlochans and in wet hummocky morasses. There are also isolated pairs dispersed along river flows. Golden Plovers, which usually nest in only low to moderate densities in the country of the gneiss, are sometimes found in higher numbers on flats and

A blockscree birchwood in the north-west — one of the least disturbed examples of this habitat.   *Stewart Angus/NCC*

A young conifer plantation.   *David S Whitaker*

Golden Eagle and eaglet at the eyrie.   *G G and I M Bates*

The Clo Mor Cliffs — a superb seabird site.   *Ian D Pennie*

hillocks of deer grass where the peat is more shallow. On mild evenings in early May the pretty bat-flights of Common Sandpipers are usually seen and heard above the larger lochs and the fast and twisting salmon rivers. But a few pairs often nest beside small lochs in the gneiss. Common Curlews are absent from many parts of the rougher boglands, even those containing large stretches of beautiful cotton sedge. Common Snipe prefer wet grasslands to the wilder peat bogs, but cocks often drum above the edges of the flow. Lapwings are not true peatland waders but small groups often haunt natural or reclaimed fringes.

Small groups of Greylag Geese still nest on small islands or in the grassy edges of a few peatland lochs in north Sutherland. You sometimes watch them swimming with their goslings on open waters beside a road. At one of our camps these lovely geese often flew in to graze almost beside us in the early morning, sometimes wakening us with their soft honking. Teal and Mallard nest in open flows but less regularly close to rivers. The scarce Scoter, first found in Scotland in 1855, nests in isolated pairs in north-east Sutherland. Wigeon are scarce, but we have seen a rare Scaup drake swimming on a small lochan in a stony flow in the north-west. Tufted Ducks are also sometimes seen on this loch. Pairs of Red-breasted Mergansers are scattered along the salmon rivers. You watch their long and exciting sex-flights and occasionally see the spectacular courtship in which the drake seizes the duck's crown. Pied Wagtails haunt rivers in the peatlands but do not nest in high numbers. Grey Wagtails are sometimes absent from seemingly attractive haunts in the gneiss. Between 1966-70 Spotted Crakes whiplashed in a stinking bog where they probably nested, but this mire was too soft and dangerous to explore. A Water Rail also called in its depths. Grey Herons do not nest in the Sutherland peatlands but they regularly fly into the bog to stalk eels and trout.

A few powerful Great Skuas have colonised flows close to the sea. Smaller Arctic Skuas are scarce, but both kinds nest on the peat of Handa Island. Solitary pairs and small clumps of Common Gulls have nests in the flows and beside rivers and lochs; they always threaten the breeding success of their wader neighbours. Great Black-backed Gulls fly over the western rivers and peatlands. We know of a small south-eastern loch far inland where an isolated pair nests in almost every year on a small island. On another small loch almost beside it there is usually a pair of Black-throated Divers and a small colony of Common Terns sometimes nest close to the shore. Noisy Black-headed Gulls breed in solitary pairs or in small colonies beside lochs or among groups of dubhlochans.

Hen Harriers and Short-eared Owls from the conifer plantations often hunt over the nearby flows. In north-west Sutherland Merlins nest on the steep bluffs of large cliffs as well as in rank heather on the flanks of sloping banks. The family found a pair of Merlins with eggs laid on the top of a huge lump of gneiss. Greenshanks had a nest on the adjacent flow. It is exciting to watch Merlins chasing northern eggar moths and to see the Jack Merlin pass food to the female. Peregrines, with eyries in nearby cliffs, include vast tracts of bog in their hunting ranges. I have watched a tiercel work a heathery corrie almost like a harrier and then drop down and rise with a Wheatear in his talons. How terrified the Greenshanks are of hunting Peregrines! They stand on rocks out in the loch ready to dive into the water. On other cliffs overlooking the bog Golden Eagles have eyries from which they fly over the flows on the look-out for deer or sheep carrion. Buzzards are less often seen deep in the peatlands but they have built nests on rocks and in old birches around the flows. The Ospreys have returned. Sometimes you watch these grand fish-hawks plunging into the lochs, pools and salmon rivers of the Sutherland peatlands. The most successful egg predators of the peatland birds are Hooded Crows. These great survivors nest in small trees in river gullies or on wooded or rocky bluffs. The deep croak of the Raven is often heard as it passes high over the boglands. One year a family of young Ravens adopted us, hopping right up to the hut door on the scrounge for scraps and pieces. Red Grouse nest in low to moderate numbers on heathery hillocks, in tumps of grass-heath, or sometimes in rank heather close to river banks. Blackcocks now have leks and greyhens nest in plantations on the peatland edges.

The amazing Meadow Pipit, the most successful bird in most kinds of open country in Britain, is strongly represented in the great bog of Sutherland. Its numbers fluctuate greatly from year to year, but there are few flows where one cannot see the cock making his lovely song-flight and parachuting to earth towards its climax. A few cock Cuckoos hold territories in the open peatlands, but in our 18 years of Greenshank study in the gneiss we have never come across a Meadow Pipit's nest with a Cuckoo's egg. Wonderful mimics of their neighbours' calls and cries, Skylarks particularly favour the shallow peat of the south-eastern flows. Their numbers also greatly vary. In the late 1970s Stonechats *chacked* on many heathery patches in the gneiss but they are now scarcer. Whinchats also occasionally favour tongues of grass and bracken on the flowland fringes.

In Sutherland the few high hills rise steeply, some almost like cups in saucers. In the north and north-east, Ben Loyal, Ben Hope, Ben Klibreck and the smaller Griams all have character. The formidable Foinaven, with its quartzite screes, the big lump of Cranstackie, and Ben Spionaidh, with its green flanks, in the north-west, are grand hills. In the west, Ben More Assynt, Quinag and Canisp, and especially Suilven, are hills of beauty and challenge.

The most characteristic bird of the Sutherland tops, the Ptarmigan, nests on a hill in the Cape Wrath peninsula on ridges between 600-1000 feet. On this remarkable hill 1000 feet is the ecological equivalent of 3700 feet in the Cairngorms. Here in early

Red-throated Diver. *Sandy Sutherland*

Black-throated Diver. *David S Whitaker*

Cormorant colony.   *Sandy Sutherland*

Hen Harrier and young at the nest.   *Sandy Sutherland*

spring on this and other Sutherland tops you listen to the frog-like croaks and sounds like anglers' reels as the cocks challenge one another.

There are few confirmed breeding records of the elusive Snow Bunting in Sutherland. In 1885 B. N. Peach, the famous geologist, watched several broods in a high corrie of Ben More Assynt. In the following year he and Lionel Hinxman, a distinguished colleague, found a nest with chicks in the same corrie. Then, in 1888, John Young recorded and took the first clutch of eggs in Sutherland. Since then there have been no confirmed breeding records from Ben More Assynt and few from other hills in Sutherland. On 13 June 1974, however, on a warm and cloudless day, David Clugston and John Mullins, two dedicated nest hunters, found a nest with five eggs on another Ben where breeding had often been suspected, but never proved. They watched the hen feeding on a scree and found the nest within 20 minutes.

The history of Dotterel in Sutherland is still more sketchy. In 1967 Margaret Suggate, a Sheffield girl, found the first recorded nest with eggs on a low hill in the north-west where, in that year, there were probably two pairs. Since 1967 Dotterels have been reported in similar habitats on five other Sutherland hills, but no further eggs or chicks have been reported. In 1981, however, two keen ornithologists watched a Dotterel running and calling on a typical whaleback in the south-east of the county.

Those who search our upland ridges sometimes make thrilling discoveries. A sharp-eyed bird watcher came upon a pair of high arctic Sanderlings in bright breeding dress displaying on the stony top of one of our Sutherland bens.

Golden Eagles regularly nest at well-spaced intervals in the uplands. Some eyries are built in huge cliffs while others are on small bluffs easily reached without ropes. Peregrines also nest on inland crags. In recent years they seem to have bred more successfully than those on sea-cliffs. Ring Ouzels nest high up in the gullies and corries and in rank heather in peatland river valleys. In early summer and late spring their piping is always evocative. On soft evenings or on windless morning the cocks challenge and advertise. Wheaters nest in the uplands and in smaller numbers among rocks and scree fields lower down. In some years they nest in high numbers in the screes of Ben Hope.

Woodlands

by David S. Whitaker

After the last great ice age, for a time, the climate was cool and dry. This was known as the Boreal Period (6800-5000 BC). Except for the mountain tops much of Sutherland, like the rest of Britain, was largely forested. Scots Pine was the dominant species at least as far north as Loch Shin. Further north and west there would have been a mixed forest of Birch and Hazel and some Pine. Towards the end of this time Sessile Oak became established on fertile south-facing slopes and Alder carr dominated the valley floors. Gradually the climate became warmer and wetter, creating conditions favourable for the growth of peat bogs. Trees were unable to regenerate freely in the wet, impoverished soils. Over much of Britain Man is charged with the destruction of the forests. Though Man had been in the north since late glacial times, the population was too sparse to have had any lasting effect on the woodland. In the Northern Highlands the change in climate was the major factor in the forest's decline.

Today only a little native Scots Pine survives in Glen Einig and Strath Carron (Page 21). Natural Oak has all but disapeared; it would have grown on fertile sites, which have long been used for agriculture. Birch woods (Page 24), though still widespread, are often restricted to steep rocky ground inaccessible to grazing animals. Many small passerine birds inhabit a typical northern or western birch wood. In spring Chaffinch and Willow Warbler are possibly the two most numerous species. Resident Great and Blue

Peregrine. *Sandy Sutherland*

Black Grouse displaying. *David S Whitaker*

Tits vie with migrant Redstarts and Spotted Flycatchers for nesting holes in the many degenerate birch stems. Long before leaf-flush Long-tailed Tits forage the woodlands for feathers with which to line their intricately woven nests. The ground vegetation is frequently heavily grazed by sheep and deer. This lack of cover for ground nesting may limit the distribution of some species such as Wood Warblers and Tree Pipits. Nesting in the tree tops, Redpolls have no such restrictions. Their noisy display flights are a common feature of many woods in spring. Attracted by the abundance of small birds, Sparrowhawks breed in most of the larger woods. Other common raptors are Buzzard, Kestrel and Tawny Owl. Long-eared Owls are less frequent but, like the Merlin, they may occasionally take over an old Hooded Crow's nest in an isolated clump of trees. Late in the evening roding Woodcock beat an invisible flight path over their territories.

Much of the finest woodland is to be found in the south and east. Here early estate planting has been linked by state forest acquisitions to form an almost continuous belt of forest from the upper Oykel to Brora. Within this region several species of birds associated with the Scottish pine forests occur. In most years as early as late January one may look for a male Scottish Crossbill singing his quiet subsong from the top of a tall pine. Nearby his chosen female may be found feeding or even nest-building. Capercaillie, re-introduced to the Highlands from Sweden, first appeared at Skibo in 1910. They became established over much of the southeast, though numbers have declined in recent years. Crested Tits have been recorded breeding in a few woods since the early fifties. Nowhere are they common: to see one in Sutherland is largely a matter of luck.

On the east coast several woods stand out from the rest. Balblair Wood south of Golspie is a fine wood of Scots Pine, owned by Sutherland Estates and managed by the Scottish Wildlife Trust as part of a nature reserve. It is of interest to the botanist, as several rare plants typical of the northern pine forest grow there. Bird watchers too will find plenty of interest. Close by, at the head of Loch Fleet, is the Mound Alderwood, possibly the finest example of an estuarine alder wood in the country. It has grown up naturally on an old beach, the result of a partly failed attempt at land reclamation after the Mound Causeway was built in 1816. Even in summer the woodland floor is waterlogged. For this reason the wood contains surprisingly few species of passerines. Travelling on the A9 between Bonar Bridge and Spinningdale one cannot fail to be impressed by a fine example of a northern oak wood growing on either side of the road. On a fine May morning it is alive with bird song and the drumming of Great Spotted Woodpecker. Here Wood Warblers are more frequent than anywhere else in the district. Tree Pipits are found along with an assortment of tits, Redstarts and flycatchers. Pied Flycatcher has been seen on several occasions but as yet has not been proved to breed there.

Since the early fifties, large areas of inland peat bog have been afforested (Page 24), mainly by the Forestry Commission. As soon as ground is ploughed and planted there is a great change in the bird population. Waders such as Greenshank, Curlew and Golden Plover cease occupation after a year or so. Other hill birds such as Meadow Pipits and Whinchats stay on in possibly greater numbers, as they benefit from the larger number of insects encouraged by the rank vegetation growing around the young trees. Hen Harriers are attracted by the abundance of prey species and suitable nest sites. In early April male harriers engage in their undulating display flights over the young conifers. In Sutherland, unlike the Orkney Islands, harriers are only rarely polygamous. Rather unexpectedly, despite much apparently suitable territory, Short-eared Owls are not common in Sutherland. Black Grouse have foresaken their traditional birch woodland habitat. Now pre-dawn leking displays frequently take place on bare ground within the forest, sometimes even on forest roads.

As the young trees close ranks, open-ground birds are squeezed out. Their places are taken by Chaffinch, Coal Tit, Redpoll and others. When the trees eventually start to bear cones, seed-eating Crossbills and Siskins move in. In the river valleys of the north and north-east the Scottish Crossbill is replaced by the Common Crossbill, an immigrant from the mainland of Europe. Rarely in Sutherland do the breeding ranges of the two species overlap. The mature stands of conifers attract most species of tree-nesting raptors. Sparrowhawks are occasionally so frequent that occupied nests are sometimes only a few hundred metres apart. Not all birds breeding in the forests are dependent on the woodland for food: in recent years several new heronries have become established.

Sutherland's woodlands form interesting and diverse habitats worth more than a passing look. Access to privately owned woods can usually be sought from their owners or estate factors. Except in times of high fire danger the Forestry Commission allow the public access, on foot, to their forests. Indeed the public are encouraged to follow the trails laid out in some areas. These follow the most scenic routes and give the visitor an opportunity to see some of the woodland birds.

Ornithological Conservation in Sutherland

by Stewart Angus

The subject of the conservation of birds is a highly emotive one, matched in wildlife circles only by the culling of seals, and leaves few people unmoved.

There are two principal organisations dealing with ornithological conservation in Sutherland who do their best to try and ensure that Man and birds can co-exist in something approaching mutual toleration.

The Nature Conservancy Council, which has an office in Golspie, is Britain's statutory nature conservation body, and manages six National Nature Reserves in the District. While most of these have some ornithological interest, in only one case was that interest of primary importance in the declaration of the NNR.

The second organisation is the Royal Society for the Protection of Birds, a national voluntary body with over 350,000 adult members — more than any political party. The RSPB manages two reserves. Handa Island is famous for its spectacular bird cliffs and attracts a large number of visitors, thus warranting a summer warden. There are regular boat trips from Tarbet, near Scourie. The second RSPB reserve is Eilean Hoan, off Loch Eriboll, which has an important wintering population of Barnacle Geese.

Perhaps the best known nature reserve in Sutherland, however, is one managed by a third voluntary organisation, the Scottish Wildlife Trust. Loch Fleet is of great importance for its wintering wildfowl and wader populations, but there is plenty to see at all times of year. A motor trail around the inlet has recently been established, but a walk to the mouth is really necessary to do the reserve justice.

Some people misunderstand the purpose of nature reserves. They are not areas where all wildlife is sacrosanct or plants and animals left to their own devices. They are areas where wildlife takes a very high priority in land management.

While legislation exists to protect individual birds, it is easiest to conserve wildlife by protecting habitat. While there is always a chance that a bird whose eggs are robbed could breed successfully in the following year, a habitat which is damaged or destroyed could lose much or all of its wildlife, perhaps permanently.

Habitat protection is easiest to achieve on nature reserves, but there is a limit to the area and number of these. In order to promote nature conservation on a wider front, the Nature Conservancy Council has notified fifty-five Sites of Special Scientific Interest (SSSI) in Sutherland District which are part of a national series, though only a small number of these would warrant SSSI status on ornithological grounds alone. The NCC is thus able to advise on the nature conservation implications of any development or major changes in land use on these important sites. Handa, Loch Fleet, the Clo Mor cliffs, and the Lower Dornoch Firth are among the areas scheduled primarily for ornithological reasons.

The two most serious threats to these prime habitats are afforestation and muirburn. The climate of Sutherland imposes an upper limit of about 250m for conifers, effectively protecting the uplands, though some of our finest bogs, including important wader and wildfowl breeding sites, could conceivably end up as Lodgepole Pine plantations. The threat of muirburn is more serious: young birds are killed in most years by late muirburn, while poorly managed (often unmanaged) burning degrades or even destroys their breeding habitat.

Many of the remaining native woodlands are threatened by heavy grazing and browsing, and there is no doubt that some very fine birchwoods will disappear within decades through lack of regeneration.

The conservation organisations are always willing to advise developers or land managers on how to minimise any impact of man on wildlife. To do this effectively they need information. The NCC and the RSPB have a number of research programmes on moorland and coastal birds in Sutherland District, and a great deal of useful data are supplied by amateurs.

Fortunately there have been no large oil spills on Sutherland's coast within the last few years. Current research is helping to identify the most important areas for birds at different times of the year, onshore and offshore. This information can be used to direct the authorities to the most important areas first when dealing with a slick.

Habitat protection alone, however, is not enough. There are still people who deliberately persecute birds, and those which are persecuted most are the most vulnerable: those at the top of the food chain, such as raptors. The dynamics of predator-prey relationships are complex, but in general predators remove only surplus stock, and it has been said that the moors with the highest raptor populations are those which yield the best game returns. Fortunately most keepers now recognise that raptors and game are compatible, and many take a keen interest in the birds on their ground. Old attitudes die hard, however, and there are still cases of birds of prey being shot or poisoned.

The illegal setting of poisoned bait is usually aimed at foxes, crows, or gulls, but frequently claims other victims: domestic animals are at risk, and the possibility of harming children cannot be ignored.

The Wildlife and Countryside Act acknowledges that some birds are pests, and allows authorised persons to kill certain species by certain methods. It is debatable whether or not this 'control' actually affects the numbers of crows or Great Black-backed Gulls. Perhaps the 'vermin' controllers, like the raptors, remove only the natural surplus.

Until recently, authorised persons were able to shoot mergansers, as they feed on salmon parr. The mortality rate of young fish is such that merganser predation, even if intense, could hardly affect stocks of adult fish. Under the Wildlife and Countryside Act, Red-breasted Mergansers may not be killed except under special licence. Dippers (listed in the old vermin returns as 'kingfishers') were once killed because they ate young fish.

Egg thieves will, perhaps, always be with us. Fortunately the Police, often with the assistance of the RSPB, have become adept at tracking down the eggers. The secrecy which surrounds nesting sites is not really a protection from these criminals: they are usually excellent ornithologists, and are often found to be in possession of very detailed maps of breeding sites.

Bird photographers have a special responsibility to keep disturbance to an absolute minimum. Photography of Schedule 1 species at the nest is illegal without a permit from the Nature Conservancy Council. The few 'cowboy' photographers who are more interested in their photographs than in the welfare of their subject, should note the words of Seton Gordon in *Wild Birds in Britain* (Batsford, 1938):—

" I should like the reader to notice especially the magnificent study of a pair of stone curlews at the nest. This photograph, the work of Mr Eric Hosking, is to my mind one of the finest nature photographs ever taken. Note the happy expressions of these very wary and unapproachable birds, and contrast them with the hunted look of birds which have been photographed by cruder

37

methods and are so nervous that they are torn between mother-love and the fear of man and all his contrivances!"

With the large number of bird-watchers in this country, and the importance of tourism locally, there is always the threat of disturbance to nesting birds. Deliberate disturbance of a nesting or nest-building bird is now illegal, but some well-meaning ornithologists insist on going too close to a nest, or keeping a bird off its nest till the eggs cool or till they are noticed by predators. A little common sense is all that is required.

The problem of disturbance is particularly acute in the case of divers. Anyone inadvertently putting a diver off its nest should move away as quickly as possible. Divers have enough problems with fluctuating water levels, and Black-throated Diver numbers are so low that every fledged chick really matters.

The relevant schedules of the Wildlife and Countryside Act 1981 are given below. All birds, their nests and eggs, are protected except for 'quarry' and so called 'pest' species. In any case of doubt, reference should be made to the Act.

SCHEDULE 1: Birds which are protected by special penalties
Part I: At all times

Avocet; Bee-eater; Bittern; Bittern, Little; Bluethroat; Brambling; Bunting, Cirl; Bunting, Lapland; Bunting, Snow; Buzzard, Honey; Chough; Corncrake; Crake, Spotted; Crossbills (all species); Curlew, Stone; Divers (all species); Dotterel; Duck, Long-tailed; Eagle, Golden; Eagle, White-tailed; Falcon, Gyr; Fieldfare; Firecrest; Garganey; Godwit, Black-tailed; Goshawk; Grebe, Black-necked; Grebe, Slavonian; Greenshank; Gull, Little; Gull, Mediterranean; Harriers (all species); Heron, Purple; Hobby; Hoopoe; Kingfisher; Kite, Red; Merlin; Oriole, Golden; Osprey; Owl, Barn; Owl, Snowy; Peregine; Petrel, Leach's; Phalarope, Red-necked; Plover, Kentish; Plover, Little Ringed; Quail, Common; Redstart, Black; Redwing; Rosefinch, Scarlet; Ruff; Sandpiper, Green; Sandpiper, Purple; Sandpiper, Wood; Scaup; Scoter, Common; Scoter, Velvet; Serin; Shorelark; Shrike, Red-backed; Spoonbill; Stilt, Black-winged; Stint, Temminck's; Swan, Bewick's; Swan, Whooper; Tern, Black; Tern, Little; Tern, Roseate; Tit, Bearded; Tit, Crested; Treecreeper, Short-toed; Warbler, Cetti's; Warbler, Dartford; Warbler, Marsh; Warbler, Savi's; Whimbrel; Woodlark; Wryneck.

Part II: During the close season

Goldeneye; Goose, Greylag (locally); Pintail.

SCHEDULE 2: Birds which may be killed or taken
Part I: Outside the close season

Capercaillie; Coot; Duck, Tufted; Gadwall; Goldeneye; Goose, Canada; Goose, Greylag; Goose, Pink-footed; Mallard; Moorhen; Pintail; Plover, Golden; Pochard; Shoveler; Snipe, Common; Teal; Wigeon; Woodcock.

Part II: By Authorised Persons at all times

Crow, Carrion/Hooded; Dove, Collared; Gull, Great Black-backed; Gull, Lesser Black-backed; Gull, Herring; Jackdaw; Jay; Magpie; Pigeon, Feral; Rook; Sparrow, House; Starling; Woodpigeon.

Bird List

Compiled by Stewart Angus

RED-THROATED DIVER *Gavia stellata* (Page 28)
This is the most plentiful of the divers, breeding throughout Sutherland, though it is less numerous in the east. It nests on small lochs, pools and, less frequently, on large lochs. Small numbers winter off all coasts, particularly the east. They move to their breeding grounds from March, or even February, onwards.

BLACK-THROATED DIVER *Gavia arctica* (Page 28)
Summer visitor, breeding in small numbers on some of the larger lochs of central and western Sutherland, often at remote sites. Has been recorded breeding on very small lochans and large pools. Nest mainly on islets and, while they are vulnerable to disturbance, most breeding failures are caused by rising water levels. Small numbers are seen off the south-east coast in winter, but there are very few winter records from elsewhere in Sutherland. They move from the sea to their breeding grounds in late March.

GREAT NORTHERN DIVER *Gavia immer*
A winter visitor to all coasts, though usually most numerous in the northern inlets. There are some summer records, mainly from the west. Arrives mainly in October and remains until late May.

WHITE-BILLED DIVER *Gavia adamsii*
1, Loch Fleet   7.4.63 (dead)
1, Loch Fleet 24.3.74
1, Golspie   8.2.78 (dead)

LITTLE GREBE *Tachybaptus ruficollis*
Resident in small numbers, breeding locally throughout the District, usually on small lochs with luxuriant vegetation. Winter birds are more dispersed and may be seen on larger lochs and in estuaries.

GREAT CRESTED GREBE *Podiceps cristatus*
Occasional winter visitor to east coast, also recorded in the north and west.

RED-NECKED GREBE *Podiceps grisegena*
Winter visitor in small numbers to the east coast, mainly to Embo, where parties of up to six have been seen. There are a few records from the north and west.

SLAVONIAN GREBE *Podiceps auritus*

Winter visitor and passage migrant in small numbers to all coasts, arriving in October and leaving April. Most records are from the south-east, though Balnakeil and the Kyle of Tongue are also favoured localities. Parties of up to 30 have been seen from Embo. First bred in Sutherland in 1929, but has not nested for many years.

BLACK-NECKED GREBE *Podiceps nigricollis*

Scarce winter visitor and passage migrant. Most records are from the Embo and Dornoch coasts. There is one record from the west coast, from Stoer in August 1962.

FULMAR *Fulmarus glacialis*

First bred in Sutherland on the Clo Mor cliffs in 1897, reaching Handa in 1902, and now breeding on all our coasts, with an estimated 5000 occupied sites on the Clo Mor, and about 3000 on Handa. Inland colonies occur at Carrol Rock in Strathbrora, and in several places in Strathfleet. Has bred on the 'artificial cliff' of Dunrobin Castle. Has also occupied rook nests at Golspie and Skelbo, though breeding has not been proved in these. Though common residents, they move offshore for short periods in mid-winter, especially during stormy weather. Occasional 'blue phase' birds have been seen, at Faraid Head, Whiten Head, Handa, and Eddrachillis Bay, but there is no record of such a bird breeding in Sutherland.

Fulmar   *R V Collier*

CORY'S SHEARWATER *Calonectris diomedea*
  Scarce autumn passage migrant.
  1, 20 miles NW of Stoer   4.10.73
  1, Brora   26.9.76 flying north
  1, Loch Fleet   30.8.79 flying north

GREAT SHEARWATER *Puffinus gravis*
  1, Eilean nan Ron   10.8.62
  1, Handa   1.9.73 flying south
  2, Brora   26.9.76 flying north

SOOTY SHEARWATER *Puffinus griseus*
  Autumn passage migrant recorded from all coasts, but most frequent on the north coast, flying west. Typical numbers are 8/hour, with a noteworthy peak of 430/hr off Brora on 26.9.76, flying north. Dates range from 5th August to 1st October. Records of single birds at Brora on 27.1.79 (freshly dead) and at Littleferry on 2.3.79 (dead a month) are puzzling as they should have been in the southern hemisphere on these dates.

MANX SHEARWATER *Puffinus puffinus*
  Passage migrant in small numbers which is most often seen on the autumn passage, though there are many spring and several summer records. Maximum numbers recorded: 327/hr flying west off Faraid Head, 15.4.72.

STORM PETREL *Hydrobates pelagicus*
  There are breeding colonies on Eilean nan Ron and Eilean Hoan, off the north coast, but neither has been counted. Breeding has been suspected on Faraid Head and, in the past, on the Badcall Islands. Birds on passage have been sighted from headlands and islands such as Handa. Exhausted birds may be blown inland in severe weather.

LEACH'S PETREL *Oceanodroma leucorhoa*
  Occasional birds may be seen from the coast. Severe storms may bring exhausted birds inland, e.g. 1, Achfary, 16.11.71 in NW gale.

GANNET *Sula bassana*
  A frequent sight from all coasts, especially in stormy weather. Most frequent off the north coast, and most records from the east

come from north of Helmsdale. Typical numbers at peak times are 200/hr., with a maximum of 700/hr. off Faraid Head. The nearest breeding colony is at Sule Stack, about 50km off the north coast.

CORMORANT *Phalacrocorax carbo* (Page 29)

There are old records of nesting in trees on the shores of the Dornoch Firth, but they ceased to breed there in about 1922. A few pairs nest on the east coast near the boundary with Caithness, at the southern extremity of one of the largest colonies in Britain. Most of the 100 or so breeding pairs of Sutherland nest on the west coast, mainly on small offshore islands such as Bulgach and the Badcalls. There are also small colonies at Faraid Head and Eilean nan Ron on the north coast. Away from breeding colonies, they may be seen on all seaboards, with up to 150 roosting on the old target at Dornoch. Occasionally seen on inland rivers and lochs.

SHAG *Phalacrocorax aristotelis*

Common resident, breeding in most parts of the north and west coasts, but restricted to the extreme north of the east coast, though sightings are frequent as far south as the Dornoch Firth. The Handa colony has declined from about 400 pairs in 1972-74 to 194 pairs in 1982.

Heron

David S Whitaker

BITTERN *Botaurus stellaris*
St John claimed to have heard Bitterns booming on the marshes at Shinness, and they were mentioned by Sir Robert Gordon in 1630. Recent records:—
1, Eriboll   20. 2.36
1, Dornoch 13.12.54

LITTLE EGRET *Egretta garzetta*
1, Bonar Bridge 22.6.54

GREY HERON *Ardea cinerea*
A fairly widespread resident. Colonies in conifers are known from south-east and central Sutherland, and they seem to be about to colonise some northern conifer plantations. There were formerly colonies at several sites around Loch Fleet but, contrary to local opinion, they have never bred in the Mound Alderwoods. There are small colonies scattered along much of the west coast, often located on cliffs. They are frequently seen feeding some distance from heronries, particularly in winter, when there seems to be a general dispersal of juveniles.

BLACK STORK *Ciconia nigra*
1, Loch Brora 18.5.77

WHITE STORK *Ciconia ciconia*
1, Eriboll   13.5.72
1, Dalchork, Lairg 21-23.4.75
1, Durness   15-20.5.77
1, Melvich   17-18.4.79

GLOSSY IBIS *Plegadis falcinellus*
1, Cambusavie 3.12.62

SPOONBILL *Platalea leucorodia*
1, immature, Loch Fleet 7.12.75—20.1.76

CHILEAN FLAMINGO *Phoenicopterus chilensis*
1, Dornoch mudflats 8.8.—21.10.76 Escape

MUTE SWAN *Cygnus olor*
Resident in small numbers, with 20-50 pairs breeding in the south-east. The chief localities are the Kyle of Sutherland, Skibo, Loch Fleet/Mound and Loch Brora. Rarely seen west of Loch Shin or north of Loch Brora.

BEWICK'S SWAN *Cygnus columbianus*
1, Altnaharra 1879

WHOOPER SWAN *Cygnus cygnus*

Regular passage migrant to all parts of the District, and winter visitor to the east, arriving in October (some in late September) and leaving in April, with stragglers into May. Tends to frequent tidal flats and the richer inland lochs such as Loch Dola, with parties of up to 40 (exceptionally 50) recorded. Small parties are frequently seen feeding in fields just south of Golspie. There are a few summer records.

Whooper Swan

David S Whitaker

BEAN GOOSE *Anser fabalis*

1, Loch Fleet 10.3.77

PINK-FOOTED GOOSE *Anser brachyrhynchus*

Common passage migrant, with many parties of up to 200 passing through.

WHITE-FRONTED GOOSE *Anser albifrons*

Scarce passage migrant: scattered records.
200, Loch Truderscaig 5.5.79, is exceptional.

GREYLAG GOOSE *Anser anser*

This species has enjoyed mixed fortunes in Sutherland, with several marked decreases and increases over the last 150 years. It is presently a not uncommon resident, breeding at scattered localities throughout the District. There is a feral flock of about 100 on Loch Brora, derived from an introduction of pure Scottish stock in 1937, which has interbred with wild birds in the surrounding area. There is another feral flock at Spinningdale. Also a common winter visitor and passage migrant. Flocks of over 500 are commonplace at passage times, and over 1000 birds have been recorded in 1 hour at Handa.

Greylag Goose   *Sally Orr*

SNOW GOOSE *Anser caerulescens*
1, Kyle of Sutherland   23.4.71: with Pink-footed Geese
1, Melness   10.6.73
2, Mudale River   1.6.74
1, Badanloch   5.7.75: Lesser, with Greylags
1, Scourie   22.1.81: Blue, with Barnacle Geese

CANADA GOOSE *Branta canadensis*
1, Kyle of Tongue   29.7.75
1, Melvich   29.7.75 (same bird)
5, Bonar Bridge   31.5.78

BARNACLE GOOSE *Branta leucopsis*

Winter visitor to the north and west coasts, but rarer on the east. The most favoured localities in the west are Eilean Chrona, Stoer; and Eilean nan Roin Mor, west of Kinlochbervie, which have a combined population of 150-250. Eilean nan Ron and Eilean Hoan are the main centres in the north, together holding 350-550 birds. Birds from these islands frequently turn up on the adjacent coast.

Barnacle Goose   *David S Whitaker*

BRENT GOOSE *Branta bernicla*

Though formerly a fairly common winter visitor, only occasionally seen nowadays. Recent records:—

2, Dornoch	30.12.78 (dark breasted)	
1, Dornoch/L. Fleet	1979-80 winter	
20, Tongue	5.10.80	
17, Kyle of Tongue	6.9.81 (light breasted)	

RUDDY SHELDUCK *Tadorna ferruginea*
    5, Durness 20.6.1892: First Scottish record.
    Two other flocks of 10 and 14 were seen in Durness in the following fortnight.

SHELDUCK *Tadorna tadorna*
    Breeds in good numbers around the sandy inlets of the north and east coasts, and occasionally in the west. Returns from its moulting grounds in December. Up to 160 may be seen in Loch Fleet in winter.

WIGEON *Anas penelope*
    First recorded breeding in Sutherland in 1834, and now nests thinly on the pool systems of inland bogs, especially in remote areas. There are large numbers of visitors in winter, particularly on the south-east coast, where up to 12,000 birds have been recorded on the north side of the Dornoch Firth. Up to 2750 have been recorded on Loch Fleet. Numbers in other areas are much lower, e.g. 100 at Loch Shin, 30-40 Kyle of Tongue.

GADWALL *Anas strepera*
    Has bred sporadically since 1913, but is still a scarce sight in summer, when most of the records are from the north coast. There are also winter visitors to north and east coasts, but numbers are very low, with up to 6 recorded at peak times on the Skibo estuary.

TEAL *Anas crecca*
    Breeds in small numbers on the pool systems of east and central Sutherland, becoming scarcer westwards. Seems to be restricted to the east coast in winter, when up to 1200 have been seen at Skibo, and up to 510 on Loch Fleet.
    There are two records of the Green-winged Teal *A.c. carolinensis*:—
    1, Culrain 7.6.74
    1, Loch Fleet 23-31.12.78

MALLARD *Anas platyrhynchos*
    Common resident, breeding throughout the District. Numbers are swollen by visitors in winter, when small parties may be seen in the bays of the west coast, and up to 600 on the eastern firths. Some birds prefer to winter on fresh water, remaining even when the lochs are partially frozen.

PINTAIL *Anas acuta*
    Up to 200 have been seen on the northern Dornoch Firth, where they gather in autumn, but typical numbers on this side of

the firth rarely exceed 50. Occasionally seen on Loch Fleet. Breeding has been reported from a few widely scattered lochs.

GARGANEY *Anas querquedula*
Pair, Stoer 10.5.77

SHOVELER *Anas clypeata*
Occasional passage migrant and winter visitor, mainly to the east, but also recorded in the north and west. There is a very old breeding record (1895).

POCHARD *Aythya ferina*
Winter visitor in very small numbers, mainly to the east coast. Occasionally seen in summer, and has bred in recent years.

RING-NECKED DUCK *Aythya collaris*
Male, Durness 28.6.77
Male, Loch Hope 18.2.78
Male, Bettyhill, various dates 14.4.79 - 6.6.79
Male, Durness 7.11.80
Possibly all records refer to the same bird.

TUFTED DUCK *Aythya fuligula*
About 20 pairs nest on the limestone lochs of north-west Sutherland, and a few pairs breed at scattered localities elsewhere in the District. Winter visitor to the Dornoch Firth, with up to 220 at Skibo and up to 150 on the Kyle of Sutherland.

SCAUP *Aythya marila*
Winter visitor in very small numbers to Loch Fleet and the northern Dornoch Firth. Scattered summer records from fresh waters and coast. Has bred.

EIDER *Somateria mollissima* (Page 10)
First recorded breeding at Tongue in 1848, and had spread throughout the west by the turn of the century. The first breeding record from the east coast was 1915 or 1916, and there was only isolated nesting there till the late 1950s. Has increased consistently, and is now a common resident, breeding on all coasts. Large 'rafts' are often seen offshore, even in summer, often with one sex outnumbering the other. These offshore flocks often include several hundred birds, and up to 3000 have been recorded at the mouth of Loch Fleet in autumn. Also winter visitor. Occasional albino and melanic birds have been recorded.

Oystercatcher. *David S Whitaker*

Ringed Plover. *Sandy Sutherland*

KING EIDER *Somateria spectabilis*

A male first appeared off the east coast on 17.11.73 and has probably been present ever since. Up to 3 have been recorded on spring passage, and two drakes were present throughout 1979. Usually seen between Loch Fleet and Embo, but recorded as far north as Brora, and south to the Dornoch Firth. Usually with common Eiders, and most obvious between October and May.

King Eider   *David S Whitaker*

STELLER'S EIDER *Polysticta stelleri*
1, Loch Fleet 22.9.59

LONG-TAILED DUCK *Clangula hyemalis*

Fairly common winter visitor to east and north coasts, but uncommon in the west. Arrives in mid-October and leaves in April, with stragglers into June. Many of the later birds are in summer plumage. In the mid-seventies, counts of up to 2000 were commonplace on the east coast, and 4000 have been recorded. Average numbers are now about 600. Similarly, in the north, the typical flock size off the Naver and Borgie estuaries has declined from 100 to 10. A winter roost of about 4000 birds was discovered off Brora in early 1982.

COMMON SCOTER *Melanitta nigra*

Small numbers breed on inland bogs, usually in remote areas, particularly in the north-east. Small numbers of non-breeders are also present in summer, but mainly a winter visitor, arriving in late August and leaving in March. Records from the north and west seldom involve more than a few birds, but flocks of up to 1000 have been recorded off Loch Fleet, and up to 7000 in the Dornoch Firth, though numbers have been lower in recent years.

SURF SCOTER *Melanitta perspicillata*
1-2 males have wintered off Loch Fleet in several years since 1974. First recorded 21.3.74. Extreme dates 5.11.75 and 22.4.76.
Male, Handa 1 - 8.6.78

VELVET SCOTER *Melanitta fusca*
Winter visitor to east coast, with very small numbers recorded in the west, and passage migrant on the north coast. Most of the east coast birds are seen from Brora southwards, with the best figures (200-500) recorded from Dornoch, Embo, and between Golspie and Loch Fleet. Arrives in October and leaves in May. There are a few summer records.

Long-tailed Duck   *David S Whitaker*

GOLDENEYE *Bucephala clangula*
Winter visitor in small numbers, arriving in October and leaving in May. Some birds remain over summer and displays and even matings have been witnessed, but there are no breeding records.

Lapwing.   *Sandy Sutherland*

Curlew.   *David S Whitaker*

Great Black-backed Gull and chick. *Sandy Sutherland*

Sandwich Tern. *David S Whitaker*

Though they may be seen throughout the District, they are scarcer (but regular) in the west, and are most numerous on the eastern inlets. Most reports are of singles or parties of up to six birds, though larger groups (25-46) have been seen at Loch Fleet and the Kyle of Sutherland.

Goldeneye   R V Collier

SMEW *Mergus albellus*
Male, Laxford 24.2.82

RED-BREASTED MERGANSER *Mergus serrator*
Resident in fair numbers, breeding throughout the District on fresh water and sea lochs. Mergansers are a common sight offshore in winter, when up to 1000 have been seen off Dornoch, and up to 250 in the Kyle of Tongue.

GOOSANDER *Mergus merganser*
Resident, breeding in small numbers, mainly in the north and west, frequenting the larger rivers. Occasionally seen in the east, especially on the Kyle of Sutherland.

RED KITE *Milvus milvus*
Bred in Sutherland as late as 1860. Only one recent record:—
1, Scourie 19.3.69

WHITE-TAILED EAGLE *Haliaeetus albicilla*

At one time commoner than the Golden Eagle, breeding as far inland as Ben Hee, but last bred in Sutherland in 1901. The only recent record is of an immature bird, seen at Bettyhill on 27.4.80. This almost certainly came from Rhum, where the Nature Conservancy Council is attempting to re-introduce them.

HEN HARRIER *Circus cyaneus* (Page 29)

Though not uncommon in the nineteenth century, they were persecuted to the extent that they had died out by the turn of the century. They returned in 1945, and bred in the following year. They have nested regularly ever since, preferring young conifer plantations, but also breeding on open moors. Common summer visitor, breeding in most areas but scarcer in the west. A few remain over winter, mainly in the east.

MONTAGU'S HARRIER *Circus pygargus*

Male, Handa 23.5.79   First Scottish record since 26.5.63

GOSHAWK *Accipiter gentilis*

There have been a few recent sightings from widely scattered areas, including a courtship display and the carrying of food.

SPARROWHAWK *Accipiter nisus*

Well distributed resident, breeding in wooded areas.

BUZZARD *Buteo buteo*

Fairly common resident, breeding in most parts of the District. Scarcer in central Sutherland and the Strath of Kildonan.

ROUGH-LEGGED BUZZARD *Buteo lagopus*

1, Kyle of Durness 18. 9.65
1, Loch Loyal   11.11.69
1, Embo   19. 5.76
1, Loch Buidhe   14. 8.76

GOLDEN EAGLE *Aquila chrysaetos* (Page 25)

Resident, breeding in small numbers in remoter parts of the District.

OSPREY *Pandion haliaetus*

Summer visitor in very small numbers, usually arriving in April and leaving in August, with passage into September. Ospreys have been sighted in most parts of the District, but are most frequent in the south-east. Bred in west Sutherland in the earlier half of the last century. Has bred in recent years.

Little Tern with chick.   *David S Whitaker*

Black Guillemot.   *Sandy Sutherland*

Long-eared Owl. *David S Whitaker*

Wood Warbler. *David S Whitaker*

GYRFALCON *Falco rusticolus*
There are two 20th century records of birds of the Greenland race, both shot: Rogart, 8.3.10 and Torrisdale, 1937.

KESTREL *Falco tinnunculus*
Present all year, breeding commonly throughout the District. Though most of our birds are summer visitors, a number remain in coastal areas over winter.

RED-FOOTED FALCON *Falco vespertinus*
1, Loch Loyal   5.7.67
1, Kyle of Durness   22.7.67
1, Meikle Ferry, Dornoch 1.5.73

MERLIN *Falco columbarius* (Back cover)
Summer visitor and resident in fairly small numbers, breeding in suitable habitats throughout the District. Usually nests on cliffs or in disused crow nests.

HOBBY *Falco subbuteo*
1, Strathnaver   12.9.72
1, Skelbo   25.9.77
1, Bonar Bridge   29.9.81

PEREGRINE *Falco peregrinus* (Page 32)
Resident and summer visitor in small numbers, nesting in suitable localities throughout the District, but breeding success is low in some areas. Lowland pairs remain over winter, but all the young, and some of the adults from upland sites, leave.

RED GROUSE *Lagopus lagopus*
Common resident, breeding on moorland throughout the District, but scarcer in the west.

PTARMIGAN *Lagopus mutus*
Resident, breeding in fluctuating numbers in central, northern and western Sutherland, and on one peak in the east. Breeds at much lower altitudes in the far north-west, where it has been seen at an elevation of 200m.

BLACK GROUSE *Tetrao tetrix* (Page 32)
Resident in small numbers, breeding locally in suitable habitat throughout the District. Has colonised some new conifer planta-tions.

CAPERCAILLIE *Tetrao urogallus*
Very scarce resident, breeding in old Scots Pines in the extreme south-east. Absent elsewhere.

RED-LEGGED PARTRIDGE *Alectoris rufa*
Thirty birds were introduced to Rosehall in 1970.

GREY PARTRIDGE *Perdix perdix*
Resident, breeding on farmland in east Sutherland and at Altnaharra and Melvich. Uncommon outside these areas, and virtually absent from the west.

QUAIL *Coturnix coturnix*
Irregular summer visitor in very small numbers, recorded in several widely scattered localities. Though birds have been heard calling, breeding has not been confirmed in recent years.

PHEASANT *Phasianus colchicus*
Fairly common resident in east, central, and northern Sutherland. First introduced in 1841, to Skibo.

WATER RAIL *Rallus aquaticus*
Scarce winter visitor (November-March), mainly to the Dornoch area, but recorded elsewhere. Has been heard calling in West Sutherland.

SPOTTED CRAKE *Porzana porzana*
Birds were heard calling in a marsh in west Sutherland between late April and early August, 1966-70.

CORNCRAKE *Crex crex*
Though formerly a fairly common summer visitor to agricultural land, numbers have decreased considerably over recent years, even in the west. Now largely confined as a breeding species to croft land in the north-west, though there are scattered pairs elsewhere, including one possibly breeding near Dornoch. 38-40 pairs are believed to have bred in Sutherland in 1978-79. Arrives from mid-May onwards, and leaves in late July.

MOORHEN *Gallinula chloropus*
Uncommon resident, breeding on lochs with luxuriant vegetation in the north and south-east, and locally in the west.

COOT *Fulica atra*
A few pairs breed in south-east Sutherland. Occasionally seen in the west and north-west, where it has bred.

Crested Tit carrying food.   *David S Whitaker*

Raven with young.   *Sandy Sutherland*

Siskin.   *David S Whitaker*

Redpoll with young.   *David S Whitaker*

CRANE *Grus grus*
1, Lothbeg Point   6.8.58
1, Oldshoremore   20-28.6.69

OYSTERCATCHER *Haematopus ostralegus* (Page 49)
Present all year, breeding throughout the District, often many miles from the sea. Breeding density in suitable habitat in the south-east 12.6 pairs/km^2. Also common winter visitor and passage migrant, the former being mainly Scottish birds, with flocks of up to 100 on the west coast and up to 200 in the north. Large winter roosts are common in the eastern inlets, with up to 1800 on Loch Fleet and 2000 on the northern Dornoch Firth.

BLACK-WINGED STILT *Himantopus himantopus*
1, Gordonbush   20.4.53

RINGED PLOVER *Charadrius hiaticula* (Page 49)
Present all year, breeding in good numbers on all flat coasts, and on the shores of the larger inland lochs. Also passage migrant.

DOTTEREL *Charadrius morinellus*
Scarce summer visitor and passage migrant, arriving in May and leaving in August. Bred successfully in 1967, and single birds or pairs have been seen on other peaks.

GOLDEN PLOVER *Pluvialis apricaria*
Summer visitor, breeding on moorland throughout the District, though breeding densities are generally lower westwards. Numbers fluctuate but are usually good. Flocks of non-breeders are occasionally recorded in summer. Small numbers are occasionally seen on the shore in winter — mainly in the east.

GREY PLOVER *Pluvialis squatarola*
Winter visitor and passage migrant to the east coast, arriving in early September and leaving in March, with passage into April. Migrants are occasionally seen on north and west coasts. Parties of up to 25 (exceptionally 145) have been seen on the Dornoch coast, with small numbers recently on Loch Fleet and the adjacent coast. First arrivals are often in summer plumage.

LAPWING *Vanellus vanellus* (Page 52)
Breeds commonly in most areas, but scarce and local in the west. The breeding population in the north collapsed in the early seventies, and is only slowly recovering. Breeding density on suitable habitat in the south-east was 42 pairs/km^2 in 1981. Also a winter visitor, mainly to the east, though sometimes seen on other

coasts. Flocks of over 800 have been seen on the eastern inlets. Numbers peak on the east coast in very cold weather and at times of passage. Return to breeding areas in February or early March.

KNOT *Calidris canutus*
Winter visitor to east coast and, to a lesser extent, to the north coast. Arrives from late August to November (bulk in October) and leaves from March to May. Passage migrant to all coasts. Though seen all along the east coast, the largest flocks are usually to be seen in the outer Dornoch Firth, where flocks of up to 3000 have been reported from Dornoch Point. There are a few summer records, some of birds in breeding plumage.

SANDERLING *Calidris alba*
Passage migrant and winter visitor in small numbers, but records for all months except March and April. Most of the records between May and September are from the west and north-west, where the most favoured locality seems to be Balnakeil. Most of the winter records (Oct-Feb) are from the east coast — mainly Brora, with the occasional record from the north. Most sightings involve less than 20 birds (max 50). Pair displayed on hill 15.6.73

LITTLE STINT *Calidris minuta*
Scarce but regular passage migrant to east coast. Rare visitor to north and west coasts. Recorded mainly on autumn passage. Exceptional peak of 230, Dornoch, 21.8.65.

TEMMINCK'S STINT *Calidris temminckii*
Single bird distracting on suitable habitat, 29.5.62
1, Handa 2.6.76

WHITE-RUMPED SANDPIPER *Calidris fuscicollis*
1, Dornoch 23.10.77

PECTORAL SANDPIPER *Calidris melanotos*
1, Handa 25-28.7.75

CURLEW SANDPIPER *Calidris ferruginea*
Scarce and irregular passage migrant on the east coast (usually 3-4 birds, autumn). Rarely recorded on other coasts.

PURPLE SANDPIPER *Calidris maritima*
Winter visitor, mainly to the east coast, where they are most often seen on the rocks at Brora and Embo. Also passage migrant on all coasts. Arrives in late October and leaves by late April. Peak number 140, Brora.

Scottish Crossbills: the cock (right) is feeding a female with young.

DUNLIN *Calidris alpina*

Summer visitor, breeding in fair numbers on moorland in many parts of the District, and occasionally in coastal localities. Also common winter visitor, mainly to the east coast, where up to 3000 have been seen at Dornoch and up to 1300 on Loch Fleet. Also passage migrant on all coasts.

STILT SANDPIPER *Micropalama himantopus*
1, Dornoch 18.4.70

First Scottish record, and first spring record for Britain.

BUFF-BREASTED SANDPIPER *Tryngites subruficollis*
1, Dornoch Point 25.9.60. Fourth Scottish record.

RUFF *Philomachus pugnax*

Scarce but regular autumn passage migrant to coastal areas in the east, recorded as far inland as Ardgay. Also recorded from Handa and the Kyle of Tongue.

Female, Dornoch Point, 25-29.4.63 is the only spring record.

JACK SNIPE *Lymnocryptes minimus*

Winter visitor in small numbers, arriving in October and leaving in April, though most frequently recorded in the earlier half of winter. Not infrequent on wet moorlands in late autumn. Driven down to coast in hard weather.

SNIPE *Gallinago gallinago*

Present all year, breeding throughout the District, and forming small flocks outside the breeding season.

WOODCOCK *Scolopax rusticola*

Fairly common resident, breeding locally in both natural and plantation woodland throughout the District. Has been known to breed on moorland up to 3km from trees. Numbers are swollen in winter by visitors.

BLACK-TAILED GODWIT *Limosa limosa*

Uncommon passage migrant and winter visitor. Most of the records are of single birds (max. 4), and the localities are widely scattered, though there is some evidence of a preference for the Kyle of Tongue and some of the larger inland lochs. The spring passage seems to take place mainly in the latter half of May, and the autumn in late August and early September. There are records for all the summer months.

BAR-TAILED GODWIT *Limosa lapponica*

Passage migrant to all coasts. Also winter visitor, with 300-2000 at Dornoch Point and Brora at peak times, with smaller numbers elsewhere. Up to 50 (usually about 6) winter on the Kyle of Tongue. There are a few summer records of birds in breeding plumage.

WHIMBREL *Numenius phaeopus*
Passage migrant in small numbers, and scarce summer visitor. Bred in 1961 and 1973.

CURLEW *Numenius arquata* (Page 52)
Common resident, breeding throughout the District, but less frequent in the west. Breeding density was 7 pairs/km^2 in suitable habitat in the south-east in 1981. Flocks, sometimes numbering more than 300 birds, are frequent outside the breeding season.

SPOTTED REDSHANK *Tringa erythropus*
Scattered autumn records from the east coast, mainly from the Dornoch coast. 1, Eilean nan Ron, 16.8.62 is the only record away from the east coast. All records have occurred between mid-August and November except 2, Dornoch, 24.4.66.

REDSHANK *Tringa totanus*
Present all year, breeding throughout the District, though less frequent in the west, particularly the north-west. Breeding density was 5 pairs/km^2 on suitable habitat in the south-east in 1981. Flocks of up to 90 have been seen on passage in the west. Up to 400 winter on Loch Fleet, and 75-100 on the Dornoch Firth. Many of the wintering birds are from Iceland.

GREENSHANK *Tringa nebularia* (Front cover)
Summer visitor: widely spread in small numbers. Breeds on suitable moors and peat bogs throughout the District, though much scarcer in the south and south-east. Soon after breeding some families move from peatland to the edges of fresh-water lochs. Sutherland is the breeding headquarters of this species, with an estimated breeding population of 340-380 pairs. Greenshanks also occur as passage migrants on all coasts, and sometimes inland, while very small numbers are recorded from time to time during winter on the north and east coasts.

LESSER YELLOWLEGS *Tringa flavipes*
1, Dornoch 31.8-7.9.80.

GREEN SANDPIPER *Tringa ochropus*
Scarce, irregular passage migrant. Four records from the west coast, all spring; 7 recent records east coast, all autumn. Pair beside loch 25.6.68.

WOOD SANDPIPER *Tringa glareola*
Very scarce summer visitor, with pairs occasionally breeding on wet ground in the north. First recorded breeding in 1959 (first time in Scotland). Has sung and displayed in other parts of the District. Also occasional passage migrant, e.g. 1. Dornoch, 13.8.74.

COMMON SANDPIPER *Actitis hypoleucos*
Common summer visitor, arriving in April and leaving in August. Breeds throughout the District, usually near fresh-water lochs with stony shores and their islands, but also on river banks and ridges and hillocks close to rivers, and by the sea. In the south-east in 1981 there were 0.9 pairs/km.

Common Sandpiper   *David S Whitaker*

TURNSTONE *Arenaria interpres*
Passage migrant and winter visitor to all coasts, arriving from mid-July onwards, and leaving as late as the end of May. Typical flock sizes are 8-12 on the west, up to 30 in the north, and 30-150 in the east, in spite of the comparative lack of rocky shores on the eastern seaboard, where Brora is the most favoured locality. May have bred in recent years.

RED-NECKED PHALAROPE *Phalaropus lobatus*
Scarce passage migrant, with a few summer records. Has bred.

GREY PHALAROPE *Phalaropus fulicarius*
1, Handa 3.9.73

POMARINE SKUA *Stercorarius pomarinus*
Passage migrant in small numbers to all coasts, but usually less numerous on the west. With only three previous records from Handa (comprising 8 individuals), there was a spectacular northward passage of 74 birds, in flocks of up to 13, during the first five days of May 1979. Only one of the 74 was dark phase. Of 9 seen from Embo Pier on 10.10.71, four were light phase adults and five were dark immature birds.

ARCTIC SKUA *Stercorarius parasiticus*
Passage migrant in small numbers to all coasts, but less frequent in the east. Summer visitors breed in increasing numbers on Handa, with 19 pairs there in 1982. Northward spring passage of 148, Handa, 20 April—6 May, 1979, including a flock of 12, the largest recorded in Scotland.

LONG-TAILED SKUA *Stercorarius longicaudus*
Occasional passage migrant, recorded on all coasts. Recent records:—
1, Balnakeil 24.6.73
1, Handa   14.6.79 (first for island)
1, Handa   28.5.80

GREAT SKUA *Stercorarius skua*
Summer visitor to north and west coasts, breeding on Handa and Eilean nan Ron. First seen on Handa on 6.5.59 and first bred there in 1964, with 12 pairs breeding in 1979 and increasing to 38 by 1982. Bred mainland Sutherland in 1975 and 1980. Also passage migrant to all coasts, but less common in the east.

LITTLE GULL *Larus minutus*
Recent records:—
1, Handa   2.6.72
1, Armadale 29.5.78
1, Dornoch 19.8.78

BONAPARTE'S GULL *Larus philadelphia*
1, Scourie 7.6.73

BLACK-HEADED GULL *Larus ridibundus*
Present all year, breeding throughout the north and east, often on inland lochs. Probably increasing, but still scarce in the west, where there are only a few colonies.

COMMON GULL *Larus canus*

Present all year, breeding commonly on all coasts, and also inland, often on islands in lochs.

LESSER BLACK-BACKED GULL *Larus fuscus*

Fairly common summer visitor, breeding on all coasts, but scarcer in the east. Arrives in April and leaves in September.

HERRING GULL *Larus argentatus*

Present all year, breeding commonly on all coasts, with only small numbers breeding in the interior of the District.

ICELAND GULL *Larus glaucoides*

Irregular winter visitor to all coasts in very small numbers. Most records are of immature birds, and most have been seen in February or March. Several records for May and June.

GLAUCOUS GULL *Larus hyperboreus*

Winter visitor in very small numbers to all coasts, but mainly to the east, where many of the records are from Embo and Golspie. Most birds are immatures, and occur between October and February, but there are records for all months except August.

GREAT BLACK-BACKED GULL *Larus marinus* (Page 53)

Common resident, breeding on all coasts, but scarce in the east, where only small numbers breed. 1,960 pairs bred on the coasts of north and west Sutherland in 1969-70 (12% of the Scottish population). A few pairs nest inland.

KITTIWAKE *Rissa tridactyla*

Common visitor, breeding on north and west coasts. Arrives on the cliffs from February onwards, and leaves in September, though birds may be seen offshore in winter. Operation Seafarer recorded 17,240 pairs breeding on the cliffs of Sutherland in 1969-70, the main colonies being at Handa, Clo Mor and, to a lesser extent, Eilean nan Ron. The Handa colony has increased from 7,000 pairs in 1962 to 13,000 in 1975. Flocks of up to 10,000 gather off Helmsdale and Brora in autumn, and smaller numbers may be seen off Helmsdale throughout the breeding season.

SANDWICH TERN *Sterna sandvicensis* (Page 53)

Passage migrant, recorded on all coasts, but most frequent on the east, where flocks of up to 100 have been recorded. Occasionally breeds in the south-east, and has bred in the north-west (1955, 1965 and 1973).

COMMON TERN *Sterna hirundo*

Fairly numerous summer visitor, arriving in late April and

leaving in September, with passage into October. More numerous in the east than west, but breeds on all coasts, and in a few inland colonies.

ARCTIC TERN *Sterna paradisea*
Common summer visitor, arriving in late April or early May, and leaving in September, with passage into October, or even November. Breeds in colonies on all coasts, with 610 pairs in 1969-70.

LITTLE TERN *Sterna albifrons* (Page 56)
Summer visitor in small numbers, breeding in a few coastal colonies in the east, with mixed success. Scarce on the north and west coasts, but has bred in the north.

BLACK TERN *Chlidonias niger*
1, mouth of River Naver 5.7.73.

GUILLEMOT *Uria aalge*
Common on suitable stretches of the north and west coasts, returning to the cliffs as early as late December. About 49,300 pairs bred in 1969-70 (10.7% of Scottish total). Breeds on islands on the west coast, with 25-30,000 on Handa, 9.5% of which are bridled. Small numbers may be seen off the east coast in winter.

RAZORBILL *Alca torda*
Common on suitable cliffs of the north and west from February onwards. About 14,200 pairs bred in Sutherland in 1969-70 (16.4% of Scottish population). The Handa colony has increased from 5340 in 1962 to c. 9000 in 1975. The cliffs are deserted in mid-August, but birds are present offshore up to late September. Small numbers have been seen off the east and west coasts in winter. The only Scottish record of the Northern Razorbill *Alca torda torda* is of a dead bird found at Brora on 12.3.47.

BLACK GUILLEMOT *Cepphus grylle* (Page 56)
Present all year, with 420 pairs (1969-70) breeding on the north and west coasts. Scarce winter visitor to the east coast, but may have bred there in 1981.

LITTLE AUK *Alle alle*
Occasional storm-blown or oiled birds recorded on all coasts, but most records are from the east, and all are winter or spring except 1, Dornoch 14.6.62 and 1, Achmelvich, 31.7.79 (latter in summer plumage). Also noteworthy is a bird found alive at Rogart (4 miles inland) on 17.1.70.

Razorbill

David S Whitaker

PUFFIN *Fratercula arctica*
Common summer visitor to north and west coasts, arriving in late March or early April. The Clo Mor colony is one of the largest in Britain, and an estimated 250 pairs bred on Handa in 1982. The breeding grounds are deserted in mid-August, though large

numbers may be seen offshore into September. Occasional winter visitor to all coasts.

PALLAS'S SAND GROUSE *Syrrhaptes paradoxicus*
1, Dornoch 6.6.1863.

ROCK DOVE *Columba livia*
Common resident, with pure stock breeding on north and west coasts. Scarce in the east, where mixed with feral stock. There is one inland breeding record. Flocks of up to 30 have been seen in autumn.

STOCK DOVE *Columba oenas*
Very scarce resident, breeding in the south-east. Occasionally seen in north and west.

WOODPIGEON *Columba palumbus*
Common resident breeding mainly in the north and east. Mainly a summer migrant in the west, but a few pairs breed.

COLLARED DOVE *Streptopelia decaocto*
Common resident, breeding locally throughout the District, but most numerous in the south-east, where it was first recorded from Dornoch on 27.4.64 and first bred in 1966.

TURTLE DOVE *Streptopelia turtur*
Scarce passage migrant, recorded from all parts of the District. Usually only 1-2 birds a year, mainly in June.

CUCKOO *Cuculus canorus*
Common summer visitor, breeding throughout the District. Usually arrives in the first week of May, but has been recorded as early as 23 April. Most leave by late July, with stragglers to late August. Meadow Pipit is the only fosterer recorded.

BARN OWL *Tyto alba*
Occasional visitor to the south-east, where it has bred.

SCOPS OWL *Otus scops*
1 shot near Morvich, May 1854.

SNOWY OWL *Nyctea scandiaca*
1, Whiten Head 13.4.72.

TAWNY OWL *Strix aluco*
Resident, breeding locally in mature woodland throughout the District, but scarcer in the west.

LONG-EARED OWL *Asio otus* (Page 57)

Resident in small numbers, breeding in mature woodland and occasionally in scrub or even on open ground in several widely scattered localities.

SHORT-EARED OWL *Asio flammeus*

Thinly scattered resident, breeding in east and central Sutherland, where it frequents young plantations. Scarce winter visitor to west.

NIGHTJAR *Caprimulgus europaeus*

Occasional visitor, with most records from the south-east, where it has bred.

SWIFT, *Apus apus*

Fairly common summer visitor, arriving in early May and leaving in mid-August. Breeds in south and south-east Sutherland and in one locality in the centre of the District. Birds on feeding flights have been seen in all areas but are scarce in the north and west.

KINGFISHER *Alcedo atthis*

1, Laxford Bridge   24.9.62. First for West Sutherland.
1, Skibo   12.11.66 and 26.11.66
1, Kyle of Sutherland 12.10.71
1, Dornoch   29.9.82

BEE-EATER *Merops apiaster*

1, Loth   12.9.35
1, Strath Halladale 14.8.59
1, Durness   2-4.5.66

ROLLER *Coracias garrulus*

1, Ledmore 7.6.79

HOOPOE *Upupa epops*

Recent records:—
1, Dornoch   3.10.65
1, Loch Choire 4.5.71
1, Loth   8.5.73
1, Bighouse   October 1974.

WRYNECK *Jynx torquilla*

1, Dornoch   3.9.58
1, Loch Hope 15.5.69
1, Loch Hope 12.6.69 calling
1, Glencassley 31.5.71
1, Altnaharra   6.5.75
1, Dallangwell 21.5.78

GREAT SPOTTED WOODPECKER *Dendrocopus major*
Resident in small numbers, breeding in the south and south-east and, locally, in the north and west.

SKYLARK *Alauda arvensis*
Mainly summer visitor, breeding plentifully in most parts of the District, but numbers fluctuate on the flows of the north-west. Scarce in winter, especially in the west.

SHORE LARK *Eremophila alpestris*
3, Little Ferry 19.12.76 - 19.3.77

SAND MARTIN *Riparia riparia*
Fairly common summer visitor, arriving in mid-April and leaving in late September or early October. Breeds in river banks and sand quarries in most areas, but scarce in the west.

SWALLOW *Hirundo rustica*
Common summer visitor, breeding in most areas. Arrives in mid-April and leaves in early October, though recorded as late as 24th November.

Swallow

Sally Orr

HOUSE MARTIN *Delichon urbica*
Fairly common summer visitor, arriving in late April and leav-

ing in early October, with stragglers into early November. Breeds in the south-east and locally elsewhere.

TREE PIPIT *Anthus trivialis*
Summer visitor in fairly high numbers, particularly to the south and east. Breeds in broad-leaved woodland and, less plentifully, in old open pinewoods. Arrives in late April and leaves in September.

MEADOW PIPIT *Anthus pratensis*
Abundant summer visitor, breeding in all suitable areas. Small numbers are present in winter.

ROCK PIPIT *Anthus spinoletta*
Resident in fairly high numbers, breeding on all suitable coasts, but scarce in the south-east.

YELLOW WAGTAIL *Motacilla flava*
Male, Strathy 18.5.74
Male, Balnakeil 19.5.73 (Blue-headed Wagtail)

GREY WAGTAIL *Motacilla cinerea*
Breeds in fair numbers by rivers in many parts of the District, but very scarce or absent from some rivers in the north-west. Present all year in the south-east, but rare in winter elsewhere.

Pied Wagtail   *Sally Orr*

PIED WAGTAIL *Motacilla alba*
The Pied Wagtail is a common summer visitor, breeding plen-

75

tifully in many parts of the District, but pairs are widely spaced on some rivers in the north-west. There are a few winter records.

The White Wagtail is a passage migrant to all coasts, more numerous in spring, and has bred.

WAXWING *Bombycilla garrulus*

Irregular winter visitor which has been recorded in most areas, but most of the records are from the south-east.

1, Corriemulzie 29.6.73

Waxwing

David S Whitaker

DIPPER *Cinclus cinclus*

Fairly common resident, breeding in fair but fluctuating numbers on most of our rivers. One river in the north-west has one breeding pair every 500m.

Dipper

David S Whitaker

WREN *Troglodytes troglodytes*

Abundant resident, breeding throughout the District.

DUNNOCK *Prunella modularis*

Common resident, breeding throughout the District.

ROBIN *Erithacus rubecula*
Common resident, breeding in all areas.

REDSTART *Phoenicurus phoenicurus*
Fairly common summer visitor, arriving in April and leaving in September. Breeds in broad-leaved woodland and mature pinewood in all suitable areas.

WHINCHAT *Saxicola rubetra*
Abundant summer visitor, arriving in April and leaving in September. Breeds in most areas, and is most numerous in young forestry plantations.

STONECHAT *Saxicola torquata*
Resident, breeding in most areas. Fairly abundant after a series of mild winters, but very vulnerable to hard weather.

Stonechat

David S Whitaker

WHEATEAR *Oenanthe oenanthe*
Abundant summer visitor, breeding in all areas. Arrives in late March and leaves by late October. Extreme dates: 22nd March and 7th November.

RING OUZEL *Turdus torquatus*
Summer visitor, arriving in early April and leaving in mid-October. Widespread, but may be locally numerous in some glens yet absent from others, even where suitable habitat seems to be available.

Ring Ouzel

Sally Orr

BLACKBIRD *Turdus merula*
Common resident, breeding on low ground throughout the District. Also winter visitor and passage migrant. Flocks of birds on passage may be seen on higher ground.

FIELDFARE *Turdus pilaris*
Common passage migrant to all areas, mainly in autumn. Most frequently seen in the Straths, where flocks of 200-300 have been recorded. Also scarce summer visitor, but has not been known to breed.

SONG THRUSH *Turdus philomelos*
Common summer visitor, breeding throughout the District. Very small numbers remain over winter, mainly in the south-east. Visitors arrive from January onwards.

REDWING *Turdus iliacus*

Common passage migrant to all areas, mainly in autumn. There are also small numbers of winter and summer visitors. Sometimes breeds in very small numbers. Icelandic and Continental races occur.

MISTLE THRUSH *Turdus viscivorus*

Summer visitor in good numbers, breeding in woodland, mainly birch, throughout the District, but scarce or absent from some parts of the north-west. Small numbers remain over winter.

GRASSHOPPER WARBLER *Locustella naevia*

Summer visitor in small numbers, recorded in most areas, but less frequent in the west and north-west. Arrives in mid-May and leaves in late August. Has bred in the west, and may breed in the east.

SEDGE WARBLER *Acrocephalus schoenobaenus*

Regular summer visitor, breeding in the south-east, in the north, and locally elsewhere.

ICTERINE WARBLER *Hippolais icterina*

1, Melvich 22.9.80 and 28.9.80

BARRED WARBLER *Sylvia nisoria*

Scarce autumn passage migrant on north coast.

LESSER WHITETHROAT *Sylvia curruca*

Scarce spring passage migrant. Recent records:—
1, Altnaharra 27-28.6.69
1, Altnaharra   4.6.70
1, Lairg   22.6.71
1, Dalchork   31.5.75
1, Dornoch   4.6.77

WHITETHROAT *Sylvia communis*

Summer visitor in small numbers, arriving from early May onwards, and leaving in September. Breeds in the south-east and west.

GARDEN WARBLER *Sylvia borin*

Scarce passage migrant, recorded in most areas. Regular on the north coast in autumn.

BLACKCAP *Sylvia atricapilla*

Scarce visitor, with most records October-December. Recorded from most areas, but most records from the south-east. There are a few spring and summer records.

YELLOW-BROWED WARBLER *Phylloscopus inornatus*
1, Melvich 6.10.79
1, Scourie 7.11.80

WOOD WARBLER *Phylloscopus sibilatrix* (Page 57)
Summer visitor in small numbers, breeding regularly in the south-east and occasionally elsewhere, mainly in broad-leaved woodland. There are non-breeding records from most areas. Arrives in mid-April and leaves in August.

CHIFFCHAFF *Phylloscopus collybita*
Summer visitor in small numbers, recorded from most areas. Arrives in early April and leaves in late September, with passage into late November. Has bred.

WILLOW WARBLER *Phylloscopus trochilus*
Abundant summer visitor, breeding throughout the District, mainly in woodland. Arrives in mid-April and leaves in mid-September.

GOLDCREST *Regulus regulus*
Resident, usually in good numbers, breeding in native and plantation woodland throughout the District. Vulnerable to hard winters.

FIRECREST *Regulus ignicapillus*
2, Lothmore 14.12.72 - 18.2.73
1, Melvich 11.9.80

SPOTTED FLYCATCHER *Muscicapa striata*
Fairly plentiful summer visitor, arriving in mid-May and leaving in September. Breeds in broad-leaved woodland and sparingly in old pines and plantations in most areas.

RED-BREASTED FLYCATCHER *Ficedula parva*
1, Melvich 25.10.76

PIED FLYCATCHER *Ficedula hypoleuca*
Uncommon summer visitor, recorded from most areas. Has bred in recent years.

LONG-TAILED TIT *Aegithalos caudatus*
Fairly common resident, breeding in woodland in many areas.

WILLOW TIT *Parus montanus*
1, 14 miles south of Cape Wrath 24.11.49
(*Scot. Nat.*, 65: 130)

1, Invercassley, April 1953 (*Scot. Nat.*, 65:130)
Pair, near Bonar Bridge, late April 1973
Bred Golspie area in the late 1960s.

The Cape Wrath record is usually accepted but the description suggests that it was a Blackcap. The Bonar Bridge record did not go through the 'official' system, but the observer is a very experienced ornithologist who knows the species well. The breeding record was published in the *Atlas* only after careful consideration, as Sutherland is well outside the normal breeding range, and there have been very few sightings this far north.

CRESTED TIT *Parus cristatus* (Page 60)
Very scarce resident, confined to the south-east, where a few pairs have bred regularly in pinewoods since at least 1952.
1, Clynelish 8.12.78 is northernmost record.

COAL TIT *Parus ater*
Common resident, breeding in most areas.

BLUE TIT *Parus caeruleus*
Common resident, breeding in most areas.

GREAT TIT *Parus major*
Common resident, breeding in most areas.

TREECREEPER *Certhia familiaris*
Fairly common resident, breeding in most areas, mainly in native woodland.

GOLDEN ORIOLE *Oriolus oriolus*
1, Strathnaver 30.5.72 and Altnaharra 5.6.72
1, Tongue 31.5.78

RED-BACKED SHRIKE *Lanius collurio*
1, Colaboll, Lairg 23.4.69
Male, 2 miles south of Tongue 28.5.69
1, North-west Sutherland 14.5.76
Male, Golspie 13.6.78
Male, Rosal 4.6.81

LESSER GREY SHRIKE *Lanius minor*
1, Kinbrace 21.6.76

GREAT GREY SHRIKE *Lanius excubitor*
Scarce winter visitor which may turn up anywhere, but most records are from the south-east.

JAY *Garrulus glandarius*
1, Dornoch 23.9.44
1, Borgie Forest 3.7.75

MAGPIE *Pica pica*
Formerly bred in the south-east, but exterminated in 1920. Now a scarce visitor, mainly to the south-east, but also recorded from the remoter parts of the District.

JACKDAW *Corvus monedula*
Resident, breeding throughout the District. Abundant in the south-east; scarce and local in the west.

ROOK *Corvus frugilegus*
Common resident in the east and the area around Tongue. Casual visitor elsewhere. In 1975 Sutherland had 31 rookeries with a total of 2110 nests. All but three of these lie east of Lairg. Rookeries at Dornoch and Invershin hold 400 and 330 nests respectively.
There are three large winter roosts which are shared with Jackdaws.
In 1970-71 the totals for both species were:—
Invershin   5000
Lawson Hospital, Golspie   4500
Tongue   250

CARRION/HOODED CROW *Corvus corone*
The Hooded Crow is an abundant resident, breeding throughout the District. The Carrion Crow is also resident, breeding in the south-east, but recorded in all areas.
Interbreeding between the two forms takes place in central Sutherland. There is evidence that the hybrid zone is moving north-west.

RAVEN *Corvus corax* (Page 60)
Resident in fair numbers, breeding widely, though very locally in the south-east. Flocks of up to 50 have been seen in the straths in winter.

STARLING *Sturnus vulgaris*
Common resident, breeding throughout the District. There are no permanent roosts on the north coast. Known to roost in coastal caves.

ROSE-COLOURED STARLING *Sturnus roseus*
1, Droman, Kinlochbervie 3.6.71 and Sheigra, 4.6.71
1, Balnakeil 16.6.71 (probably Kinlochbervie bird)

1, Faraid Head 9.-14.7.72
1, Scourie 31.8.72 and 28.9.72
1, Helmsdale 2.7.76
Some or all of these records may be of escapes.

HOUSE SPARROW *Passer domesticus*
Resident, breeding around habitation throughout the District.

TREE SPARROW *Passer montanus*
Scarce resident, breeding irregularly in the south-east, and only occasionally seen elsewhere.

CHAFFINCH *Fringilla coelebs*
Abundant resident, breeding throughout the District.

BRAMBLING *Fringilla montifringilla*
Rather irregular winter visitor and passage migrant, with the largest flocks (150) recorded in the south-east, but records from all areas. Occasionally birds display and sing in summer, but there is only one breeding record (1920).

GREENFINCH *Carduelis chloris*
Fairly common resident, breeding in the south-east and north. Scarce in the west.

GOLDFINCH *Carduelis carduelis*
Present all year, possibly breeding in small numbers in the south-east. There are also sightings from the north and west, mainly in winter.

SISKIN *Carduelis spinus* (Page 61)
Present all year, breeding locally in different kinds of conifer woodland in greatly fluctuating numbers. Breeds throughout the District, but is scarce in the west and north-west. Forms flocks of up to 250 in winter, and now often feeds on peanuts at bird tables in late winter.

LINNET *Carduelis cannabina*
Common resident, breeding locally, mainly in coastal areas of the east and north, and very locally in the west, where it is a summer visitor. Flocks of over 200 have been seen in autumn and winter.

TWITE *Carduelis flavirostiris*
Resident, breeding in most suitable areas, but scarcer in the south-east. Confined to low ground in winter, when flocks of several hundred have been seen.

REDPOLL *Carduelis flammea* (Page 61)

Common resident, breeding throughout the District in birch and young conifers. They winter in birch and alder woods, forming flocks of up to 200. Our birds are Lesser Redpolls *Carduelis flammea cabaret* but small numbers of the Mealy Redpoll *C.f. flammea* have occurred on passage and in winter.

CROSSBILL *Loxia curvirostra*

Resident in small numbers, breeding locally in coniferous woodland in central, south-east and north-east Sutherland, and very locally in the west. The breeding range has been known to overlap that of the Scottish Crossbill. Flocks have been noted in irruption years.

SCOTTISH CROSSBILL *Loxia scotica* (Page 64)

Resident in small numbers, breeding in old pines in the south and south-east.

TRUMPETER FINCH *Bucanetes githagineus*

1, Handa 8-9.6.71

SCARLET ROSEFINCH *Carpodacus erythrinus*

Male, Lairg 8.6—22.7.77
Male, Golspie 9-26.6.78

BULLFINCH *Pyrrhula pyrrhula*

Fairly common resident. Though seen throughout the District in summer, breeds only in the south-east and the west, and occasionally in the north. Small feeding flocks (exceptionally up to 100) form in winter.

HAWFINCH *Coccothraustes coccothraustes*

2, Cape Wrath 15.10.11
Male, near Achfary 6.7.77

LAPLAND BUNTING *Calcarius lapponicus*

1, Handa   27.5.58
7, Eilean nan Ron   9.9.62
1, Whiten Head   21.3.70
1, Sheigra 2.6.72 Male in full summer plumage
2, Strathy Point   10.9.75 Calling

SNOW BUNTING *Plectrophenax nivalis*

Regular winter visitor in small numbers to all areas, arriving in late September and leaving by mid-April. The largest winter flocks have been recorded on the coast, the largest in recent times being one of 400 at Loch Fleet on 16.11.73, though 'great many thousands' were seen at Strathy Point on 30.11.31. Also passage migrant. Broods were located on Ben More Assynt in 1885 and the first nest was found there in 1886. Birds are periodically recorded on other hills, but the only confirmed breeding record in recent years was in 1974.

PINE BUNTING *Emberiza leucocephalos*
    Male, Golspie 6-8.1.76

YELLOWHAMMER *Emberiza citrinella*
    Fairly common resident, breeding in the east and locally in the north and west.

ORTOLAN BUNTING *Emberiza hortulana*
    Male, Clo Mor 9.6.76

RUSTIC BUNTING *Emberiza rustica*
    Male, Cape Wrath 11.5.06

LITTLE BUNTING *Emberiza pusilla*
    1, Rosehall 29.12.79

REED BUNTING *Emberiza schoeniclus*
    Thinly scattered resident, breeding in marshy areas throughout the District, even in wet areas in conifer plantations.

RED-HEADED BUNTING *Emberiza bruniceps*
    Male, Scourie 13.5.72 Probable escape.
    Male, Handa 1.6.75 Probable escape.

CORN BUNTING *Miliaria calandra*
    Formerly common, this species has now become very scarce, and may no longer breed in the District. There are only 3 sightings from the Dornoch area since 1972, where 20 pairs had bred in the 1960s. Probably disappeared from the north and west by 1961.

LAZULI BUNTING *Passerina amoena*
    Male, Achfary, late May, 1974. Probably an escape.

SELECTED BIBLIOGRAPHY

ATKINSON-WILLES, G.L. (Ed.) 1963. *Wildfowl in Great Britain.* Nature Conservancy Monograph, H.M.S.O.

BAXTER, E.V. and RINTOUL, L.J. 1953. *The Birds of Scotland.* 2 vols., Oliver and Boyd, Edinburgh.

CRAMP, S., BOURNE, W.R.P. and SAUNDERS, D. 1975. *The Seabirds of Britain and Ireland.* Collins, London.

DARLING, F.F. and BOYD, J.M. 1964. *The Highlands and Islands.* Collins, London.

GORDON, R. 1813. *A Genealogical History of the Earldom of Sutherland from its Origin to the year 1630.* Constable, Edinburgh.

HARVIE-BROWN, J.A. and BUCKLEY, T.E. 1887. *A vertebrate fauna of Sutherland, Caithness and West Cromarty.* David Douglas, Edinburgh.

HARVIE-BROWN, J.A. and BUCKLEY, T.E. 1895. *A fauna of the Moray Basin.* David Douglas, Edinburgh.

HARVIE-BROWN, J.A. and MACPHERSON, H.A. 1904. *A fauna of the north-west Highlands and Skye.* David Douglas, Edinburgh.

MACDONALD, D. 1981. Birds on Loch Fleet Reserve. *Scottish Wildlife,* 17: 19-20.

MILNER, W.M.E. 1848. Birds of Sutherland, Ross-shire, etc. *Zoologist,* 6: 2014-2017.

MUDGE, G.P. and ALLEN, D.S. 1980. Wintering seaducks in the Moray and Dornoch Firths, Scotland. *Wildfowl,* 31: 123-130.

NETHERSOLE-THOMPSON, D. 1978. *Highland Birds.* H.I.D.B., Inverness.

NETHERSOLE-THOMPSON, D. and NETHERSOLE-THOMPSON, M. 1979. *Greenshanks.* Poyser, Berkhamstead.

OMAND, D. (Ed.) 1982. *The Sutherland Book.* The Northern Times, Golspie.

PENNIE, I.D. 1951. The Clo Mor bird cliffs. *Scot. Nat.,* 63: 26-32.

PENNIE, I.D. 1962. A century of bird-watching in Sutherland. *Scottish Birds,* 2: 167-192.

RATCLIFFE, D. (Ed.) 1977. *A Nature Conservation Review.* 2 vols., Cambridge University Press, Cambridge.

RATCLIFFE, D. 1979. *The Peregrine Falcon.* Poyser, Calton.

ST. JOHN, C. 1849. *A tour in Sutherlandshire.* 2 vols., Douglas, Edinburgh.

SCOTTISH BIRD REPORTS. *Scottish Birds.*

SELBY, P.J. 1836. On the quadrupeds and birds inhabiting the county of Sutherland. *Edin. New. Phil. J.,* 20: 156-161; 286-295.

SHARROCK, J.T.R. 1976. *The atlas of breeding birds in Britain and Ireland.* British Trust for Ornithology, Tring.

VOOUS, K.H. 1977. List of recent Holarctic bird species. *Ibis,* 119: 223-50; 376-406.

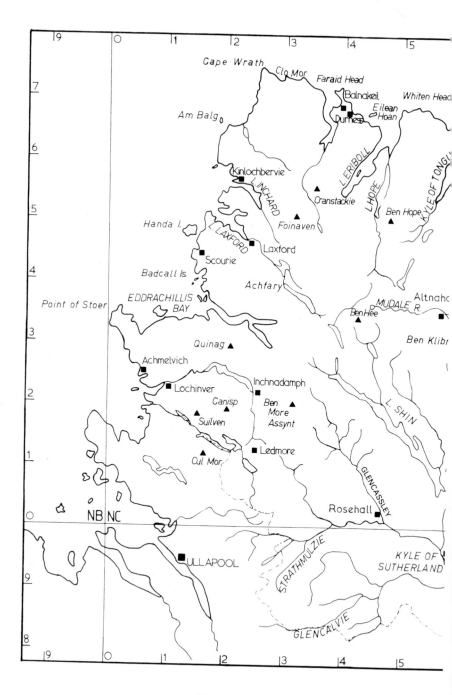

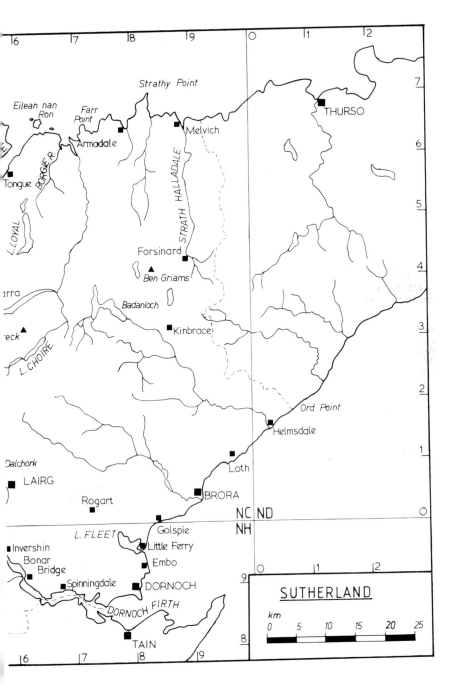

Gazetteer of Place Names

This list enables readers less familiar with Sutherland to locate places mentioned in the text. While the list may be used in conjunction with the map on the preceding pages, it should ideally be used with the Ordnance Survey 1:50000 maps. With one or two exceptions place names are as used on O.S. maps.

The National Grid reference is given after each place name. Full details of the use of grid references may be found on any O.S. map. the two letters refer to the 100 x 100 km square, most of Sutherland being in the square NC. South Sutherland is in the square NH and the extreme east is in ND.

Two-figure references following the letters locate particular 10 x 10 km squares, popularly known as '10 km squares'. The first figure is the 'easting' and the second (or third in four-figure references) is the 'northing'. e.g. Lairg is in 100 x 100 km square NC, it is in 'easting' square 5 and 'northing' square 0, and the 10 km square is thus NC50. Four figure references locate particular 1 x 1 km squares: to find the 10 km square, take the first and third figures: e.g. Achmelvich is in 1 x 1 km square NC0524 and 10 km square NC02.

References are given only to enable the place to be located on a map. They do not necessarily refer to the exact spot where birds were seen, and may locate only part of large areas such as water bodies or mountains.

Achfary	NC2939	Canisp	NC2018
Achmelvich	NC0524	Clynelish, Brora	NC8905
Altnaharra	NC5635	Clo Mor	NC37
Am Balg	NC1866	Colaboll, Lairg	NC5610
Amat	NH4790	Corriemulzie	NH39
Ardgay	NH5990	Cranstackie	NC3555
Armadale	NC7864	Culrain	NH5794
Badanloch	NC73	Dalchork, Lairg	NC51
Badcall Islands	NC14 and 13	Dallangwell, Strathy	NC8259
Balnakeil	NC3968	Dornoch Point	NH8087
Ben Griams	NC83	Drumhollistan	NC9165
Ben Hee	NC4233	Dunrobin, Golspie	NC8500
Ben Hope	NC4750	Durness	NC4067
Ben Klibreck	NC5829	Eddrachillis Bay	NC13
Ben More Assynt	NC3120	Eilean Hoan	NC4467
Ben Spionnaidh	NC3657	Eilean nan Ron	NC66
Bighouse, Melvich	NC8964	Embo	NH8192
Borgie Estuary	NC6862	Eriboll	NC46
Borgie Forest	NC65	Faraid Head	NC37
Bulgach (Am Balg)	NC1866	Farr Point	NC7164
Cambusavie	NH7796	Foinaven	NC34

Index and Check-list

Page numbers shown in **bold type** refer to the main entry for that species, other references to the text being shown in normal type. References to illustrations are given in *italics*.

92

LIST OF USEFUL ADDRESSES

Bird records should be sent to the local recorder for Sutherland, except for those from the parish of Kincardine, which should be sent to the recorder for Ross-shire. The names and addresses of the recorders for Sutherland and the adjacent counties are given below:—

Sutherland: A R Mainwood, 13 Ben Bhraggie Drive, GOLSPIE, Sutherland.
Ross-shire : R H Dennis, Landberg, North Kessock, INVERNESS, IV1 1XD.
Caithness : P M Collett, Sandyquoy, Scrabster, THURSO, Caithness.

Royal Society for the Protection of Birds,
Landberg, North Kessock, INVERNESS, IV1 1XD.
Highland Officer: Roy H Dennis.   Assistant: Roger Broad.

RSPB, 17 Regent Terrace, EDINBURGH, EH7 5BN.

Nature Conservancy Council
Sub-regional Office, Old Bank Road, GOLSPIE, Sutherland, KW10 6RS.
Assistant Regional Officer: Stewart Angus.

NCC, North-west Scotland Region, Fraser Darling House, 9 Culduthel Road, INVERNESS, IV2 4AG.
NCC Scotland Headquarters, 12 Hope Terrace, EDINBURGH, EH9 2AS.

Scottish Ornithologists Club, 21 Regent Terrace, EDINBURGH.

Scottish Wildlife Trust, 25 Johnston Terrace, EDINBURGH, EH1 2NH.
Area Representatives:
West Sutherland: Dr I D Pennie, 5 Upper Badcall, Scourie, by LAIRG, Sutherland.
East Sutherland: D Macdonald, Elmbank, DORNOCH, Sutherland.

The East Sutherland Bird Group meets monthly on Monday evenings in Golspie during the winter months, and organises field trips. The Honorary Secretary is Susan Read, An Sithean, BONAR BRIDGE, Sutherland.